Longman M

POPULATION

GEOGRAPHY

M E Witherick
Lecturer in Geography
University of Southampton

Longman
London and New York

for Penny, Lusanna and Nicholas

Longman Group UK Limited
Longman House, Burnt Mill, Harlow, Essex,
CM20 2JE, England and Associated Companies
throughout the World.

© Longman Group UK Limited 1990

First published 1990
Second impression 1993
ISBN 0 582 35586 9

Set in 10/12 pt Times, Linotron 202
Produced by Longman Singapore
Publishers (Pte) Limited
Printed in Singapore

The publisher's policy is to use paper manufactured
from sustainable forests.

British Library Cataloguing in Publication Data

Witherick M. E. (Michael Edward), 1936–
    Population geography. — (Longman modular
    geography series).
    1. Population. Geographical aspects
    I. Title
    304.6

Library of Congress Cataloging-in-Publication Data

Witherick, M. E.
    Population geography/M. E. Witherick.
    p.   cm. — (Longman modular geography series)
    Includes bibliographical references.
    ISBN 0-582-35586-9
    1. Population geography.   I. Title.   II. Series.
HB1951.W58   1990
304.6 — dc20

Contents

Preface

This modular series of nine separate but interlocking geography texts is designed primarily for sixth form students in the 1990s in the UK. The series is written by a team of authors who, with the Joint Editors, are Chief Examiners and Moderators for a number of GCE Examining Boards and have been actively involved with sixth form teaching of geography at GCE 'A', and now A/S Levels, as well as at college and university level.

In any modular system, self-standing parts are complementary to each other and to the series as a whole which caters, in its full range of systematic studies for the needs of any conventional UK geography 'A' Level syllabus. In this series, there are nine texts: three physical and three human, together with three which focus on the interfaces (a) within physical geography, (b) within human geography and (c) between physical and human geography. Thus, the traditional compartmentalisation of the subject is challenged and new interdisciplinary syllabus and educational developments anticipated. Moreover, real case-studies on global and local scales abound throughout, providing a continuing, but ordered and necessary, real-world perspective. Assignments of varying types are to be found in each chapter, providing stimulating work at the sixth form level as well as maintaining the spirit and approaches of GCSE.

Above all, this series offers a representative range of geography books, covering most of the subject, from which individuals may select their own combination for study. A combination of selected physical, human or interface texts can be tailored to suit any teaching programme and designed to meet the special requirements of a specific 'A' or 'A/S' Level syllabus, including those 'A/S' Levels which concentrate on physical or human topics alone. Again, the available expertise and preferences in any given sixth form centre could govern the selection of texts adopted for study. Such selections could favour specialisation (either in physical or human geography) or the interdisciplinary approach (based primarily on the interface volumes). The choice is yours.

Geography is a changing academic subject in a changing world, a changing society and, changing environment, creating great interest and new challenges at all educational levels. The inquisitive and illustrative style of these texts will provide sixth formers with the opportunities to learn, by self-discovery, how theory matches practice and how the local, or distant, geographies can come alive in the classroom. Geography is in a unique position, straddling the humanities and the sciences, yet maintaining a strong academic and professional identity of its own. This series of texts serves to promote and advance that identity, in both the pure and applied senses, providing a contribution to training for good citizenship, and environmental awareness, as well as perspectives on human opportunities and environmental issues the world over.

B. P. Price
J. A. Taylor
(Joint Editors)

1

Definition, Data and Distribution

WHAT IS POPULATION GEOGRAPHY?

The aim of this book is to answer this apparently simple and straightforward question and to do so by describing, explaining and exemplifying what this one branch of geography is all about. Having said that, it might seem a little strange to be bothering with this question in the opening paragraph and to be seeking, as it were, a short-cut answer to it. You will perhaps be thinking to yourself – 'If it can be done in a paragraph or two, why go to the trouble of writing a whole book on the subject?' The fact is that the question cannot possibly be answered properly within such a short space. Nonetheless, some brief introductory comments about the special character of population geography, and how it relates to the rest of geography, might go some way towards providing a rationale for the overall structure of the book and for the content of individual chapters. Brief coverage of these points should also help to get population geography into perspective by establishing its place within the subject of geography as a whole (Fig. 1.1).

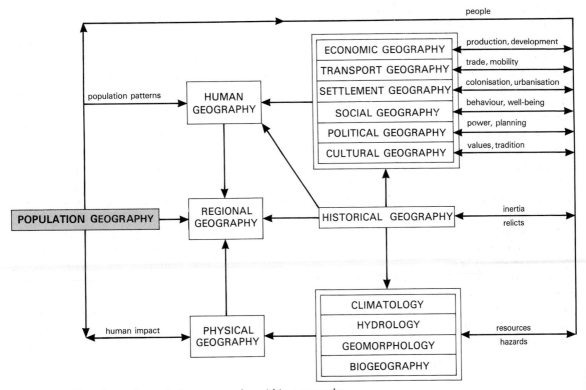

Figure 1.1 *The place of population geography within geography*

Although there is no universally accepted definition of geography, it is widely agreed that the most distinctive characteristic is its concern with what is called the *spatial dimension*. This simply means that geography, being the study of the world, is particularly interested in the way things occur over the face of the earth – be they pediments, plants or people. The occurrence of any one such thing is known as its *spatial distribution*. Geography also seeks to discover the reasons why things occur where they do in this spatial dimension. Thus, many would see the main focus of geography to be the description and explanation of spatial distributions.

It follows that much of the business of population geography is going to be about the spatial distribution of people and the various factors that interact to influence that distribution (Chapter 1). But the interest goes much further than just how *population numbers* and *population densities* vary from place to place. There is need to explore the dynamics of *natural population change*, particularly the key components of *fertility* and *mortality* (Chapter 2). The global increase in population constitutes another vital aspect of population geography. So too do the spatial variations in rates of population change, especially as countries make the *demographic transition* from high to low levels of fertility and mortality (Chapter 3). Another powerful influence on rates of population change is *migration*, the movement of people across the earth's surface, be it of settlers moving into previously uninhabited lands or commuters travelling to and from work (Chapter 4).

The legitimate concern of population geography also extends to the different dimensions of *population structure*, such as age, sex, marital status, ethnicity and household characteristics (Chapter 5). These have a bearing on population distribution and change. They also raise topical issues, such as how to cope with the demands of *silvering* (ageing) populations, matching housing supply with household characteristics, and reducing the tensions of multi-ethnic societies. Finally, there is the crucial topic of the relationship between population numbers, resources and development. An investigation of this relationship leads into what might be called the geography of hunger and of plenty (Chapter 6). But the geographer's interest in this critical relationship should not be confined to the present; it needs to be converted into concern for the future (Chapter 7). Questions about future levels of population and whether the global resource base will be able to adequately support more and more people require reliable answers and appropriate action. These then are the principal aspects or topics of population geography to be explored in this book.

Of all the systematic branches that are recognised as making up geography, it might be claimed that population geography is by far the most important, especially where human geography is concerned. After all, what is human geography if it is not about people? Indeed, it has been claimed that population numbers, densities and qualities provide the essential background for all geography. Others have expressed the significance of population geography in another way; they stress that the whole of geography relates, in some way or another, to the uneven distribution of population over the earth. If any branch of geography is not concerned with some of the causes contributing to that uneven spatial distribution, then it is likely to be studying some of the *consequences* of that unevenness.

Figure 1.1 illustrates that population geography may, with justification, be seen as occupying a strategic location within modern geography. Looking down the right-hand side of the diagram, it will be seen as interacting with the other systematic branches of human geography. For example, the *well-being* of people – a product of the relationship between population numbers, resources and development – binds together population and social geography. A common interest in the values and traditions of people provides a similar bond between population and cultural geography. Population geography also has direct links with the two other main divisions of geographical study, namely physical and regional geography. For physical geography, the link is a reciprocal but unequal one. Although the physical environment is being increasingly modified and controlled by people, it still holds the upper hand in terms of continuing to exert a powerful influence on the distribution and well-being of people. Those two dimensions (i.e. physical and human geography) also represent basic components of regional geography.

ASSIGNMENTS

---

1 Make a list of both physical and human factors whose spatial distributions figure prominently in geographical study.
2 With reference to Figure 1.1, identify and explore the ways in which population geography interacts with the other branches of human geography.
3 Exemplify some of the reciprocal relationships that exist between people and the physical environment.

SOURCES OF POPULATION DATA

The fundamental need in population geography is for accurate information about various aspects of the world's population. First, we need a reliable assessment of population numbers and a clear idea of their distribution at a range of spatial scales, from the continent to the country parish. Then there is the vital matter of population structure; that is the population's make-up as regards age and sex, marital status, ethnic origins, household size and so on. A third need is for information about population change. This is required in order to determine whether the population of an area is increasing or declining, and at what rate. It is also important to know what is causing that change. Is it due to there being more births than deaths, known as *natural increase*, or to a difference in the numbers of migrants arriving and leaving (referred to as *net migration*), or to a shift in the balance between natural increase and net migration?

For each of these broad categories, we need ideally to have data for the whole range of spatial scales; for the continents, for countries, for regions within those countries, right down to small areas within towns and country districts. Unfortunately, information in this detail is not available for all parts of the world. Even where it is available, quality and accuracy vary enormously from country to country. In nearly all cases the responsibility for collecting and publishing population data, and the control over the quality of those data, rests with national governments. The more advanced countries have the resources and organisations to collect large quantities of reliable information about their people. The supply of information relating to Third World countries is less reliable; although during the post-war period, the United Nations Organisation (UNO) has done much to improve the supply of demographic information from such countries. The UNO has also tried to achieve international standardisation by encouraging all countries to collect the same types of information about population in their *censuses*, and at the same regular intervals. At present the following aspects of population are recommended for assessment:

1 Total population and its distribution within the country.
2 Sex, age and marital status.
3 Place of birth, citizenship or nationality.
4 Mother tongue, literacy and educational qualifications.
5 Economic characteristics (occupation).
6 Residential location (urban or rural).
7 Household or family size and structure.
8 Fertility.

Coordination of the census efforts of individual countries should produce a much clearer picture of global population, both of its numbers and current characteristics. This standardisation also makes it much easier to undertake comparative studies at an international level. In addition, collecting such data on a regular and frequent basis makes it possible to monitor trends of demographic change, which is a vital aspect of population study. Thus it is that since 1801 Britain has surveyed its population once every ten years, with the exception of 1941. Other countries manage to maintain a more frequent monitoring; Japan, for example, conducts a census once every five years.

The census

Statistical data crucial to population geography may be derived in different ways. For instance, a national census may collect, collate and publish data relating to the nation's population at a given and precise time; the 1981 Census of the United Kingdom was taken at midnight on the 5/6 April, 1981. Such a census therefore yields a static snapshot of the population. Normally, the national census involves the whole of the population. Sometimes, however, it might be undertaken on a sample basis, with perhaps only 10 per cent of the total population being scrutinised. From this sample data, general conclusions about the whole population may be derived, but only within clearly defined margins of statistical error.

More fundamental than the distinction between comprehensive and sample censuses is the difference in data collection methods employed. Basically, there are two methods. By the *de facto* approach, each person is recorded at the place where he or she was found to be living at the time the census was taken. This method is followed by the British Census. By the *de jure* approach, people are counted in the census according to their normal place of residence. This approach was used in Palestine at the time of Christ's birth and today is used in the United States. Such features of population as high levels of mobility, the ownership of more than one home and homelessness make the *de jure* approach less satisfactory. Yet *de facto* enumeration tends to inflate the population totals of holiday resorts and places containing sizeable institutions such as universities and colleges, army barracks, hospitals and prisons.

Spatial units

All census data are collected initially on the basis of small areas. In Britain these are known as *enumeration districts* and represent the area covered by one census collector working on a door-to-door basis; on average they comprise between 160 and 220 households. However, when the census results are published, these small areas are usually amalgamated into larger units. In Britain, for example, the enumeration districts are aggregated into wards, which, in turn, are aggregated into local government areas of boroughs and district councils. These local government areas are generally the smallest areas for which census data are published. Information for smaller areas may be obtained from the Office of Population Censuses and Surveys (OPCS) on magnetic tape, microfilm, microfiche or computer print-out.

The areal units used in a census are a matter crucial to the geographer. Two aspects are especially significant. The first is the scale of the units and of the area being investigated. Clearly, if the study is concerned with the broad national distribution of population, then it will be sufficient to have data aggregated at a county or state level (Fig. 1.2a). If we are interested in the distribution of population within a city, then we need to have data for smaller areas. In Britain this would be data at either a ward or an enumeration district level (Fig. 1.2c). The second aspect concerns the consistency of those areal units over time. This is critical if the focus of attention is on population change, for it is then necessary to compare exactly the same area at two or more different times. In most countries local government area boundaries are periodically reviewed and redrawn, whilst enumeration districts are often completely re-jigged for each new census. This makes it exceedingly difficult to accurately monitor local population changes within towns and cities. Fortunately, in the organisation of

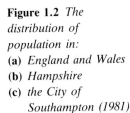

Figure 1.2 *The distribution of population in:*
(a) *England and Wales*
(b) *Hampshire*
(c) *the City of Southampton (1981)*

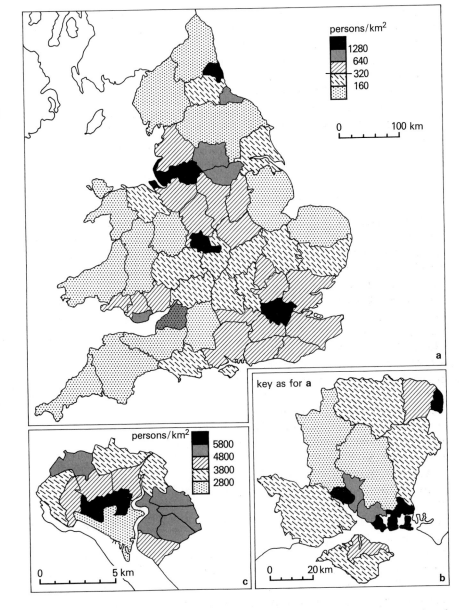

persons/km²
1280
640
320
160

0   100 km

key as for **a**

persons/km²
5800
4800
3800
2800

0   5 km

0   20 km

the 1981 British Census, every effort was made to retain the same enumeration districts as had been employed in the 1971 Census.

These same issues of the scale and consistency of areal units also arise in connection with the other principal source of population data. This is registration of the *vital statistics* of a population, and involves marriages, births, adoptions, divorces and deaths. Most governments require these events to be officially notified. Such registration has been a legal requirement in Britain ever since 1876. The advantage of such data is that they represent a continuous record of population. By contrast, the traditional census provides only an occasional or periodic snapshot of the population. On the other hand, vital registration does not normally monitor so many different aspects of the population as are covered by the average national census.

ASSIGNMENTS

4 Explore in more detail the advantages to be gained by countries from standardising the content and coordinating the timing of their censuses.

5 Compare the merits and limitations of the *de facto* and *de jure* census methods.

6 For your local area, find out about the enumeration districts used in the last census. Plot them on a large-scale map. Obtain data for those enumeration districts from your local government offices or OPCS. Analyse that data, and in particular compare your enumeration districts in terms of each of the variables.

MAPPING THE DISTRIBUTION OF POPULATION

One of the first lines of investigation by the population geographer is almost certain to be an analysis of population distribution within a given area. This might seem a simple task, but on close inspection it is soon found to be fraught with difficulties. The basic need here is to produce a map which relates people to where they actually occur on the ground. In most cases this means mapping the distribution of people in terms of their place of residence. This may be accomplished in two different ways.

Located symbols

The first method involves taking a base map of the area under investigation, probably a topographic map, and locating population on it by means of a standard symbol. This could be a dot representing a given number of people, as in Figure 1.3a. Alternatively, the symbol might be a circle whose radius is proportional to the number of people being represented, as in Figure 1.3b. A map could use both symbols; for instance, the villages might be shown by proportional symbols and the intervening scattered farmsteads and dwellings by the standard dots. This last approach

may well give a good and accurate visual portrayal of the actual distribution, though the preparation of such a map would entail much detailed investigation and a long and painstaking process of plotting.

The choropleth technique

A second strategy involves mapping the distribution in terms of the relationship between population numbers and area, a measure usually referred to as *population density*. This offers a much quicker method for representing and analysing the distribution of people, but there are some difficulties. Not least of these relates to the actual areal units to be used in the analysis. Ideally, we would like to be able to place a regular grid over our base map, count the number of people occurring in each square and then convert that number into persons per unit area (usually persons per km^2). Subsequently all the grid square values would be classified on a scale spanning from the lowest to the highest densities. Each square on the map would then be shaded according to its density class, a cartographic technique known as the *choropleth method* (Fig. 1.3c).

Use of the choropleth method in the painstaking manner just described can be a time-consuming operation, requiring detailed knowledge about the precise location of people within the study area. This may be acceptable where only a small area such as a rural parish is being investigated, but the task would be huge if population distribution at a national level were to be mapped in the same way. Thus the key to effective and efficient use of the choropleth method lies in analysing population distribution within the study area by means of appropriately-scaled subdivisions. In terms of data availability, ideally those subdivisions should coincide with one of the levels of administrative area used in the compilation of census returns or vital registrations – namely wards, parishes, counties, regions or even countries (Fig. 1.3d). So, for example, the general distribution of population in England and Wales would be

Figure 1.3 *Cartographic methods for showing the distribution of population*

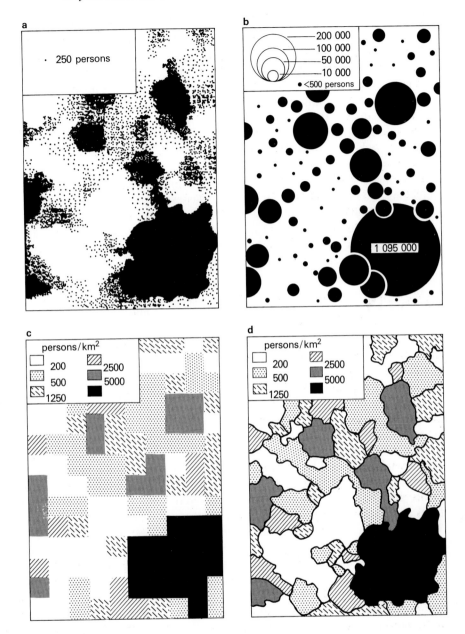

most readily mapped in terms of the average population density in each constituent county (Fig. 1.2a, p. 9); whilst an enquiry concerned with the distribution of population within a major city would most appropriately use ward or enumeration district subdivisions (Fig. 1.2c). In both cases, the final map would make use of the choropleth or shading technique to portray the range in density values.

Population density maps do, however, have limitations which should be borne in mind when it comes to their interpetation. First, no matter at what spatial scale or for what administrative areas, these maps represent average values for the chosen areal units. Mean values are generalisations which conceal spatial variations occurring within the areas for which they have been calculated. A second limitation is that the choropleth map can so easily give a false impression. This happens particularly where adjacent areas show significantly different density values (Fig. 1.3d). The map may indicate, quite erroneously, a marked break in the continuity of population distribution occurring along the boundary between the two areas, when in fact there is a smooth transition in densities.

There are also some technical problems encountered in the compilation of a population density map. These revolve around the twin questions: how many different density classes should be recognised, and how should these classes be delimited? Satisfactory answers to these questions usually involve striking a compromise between the visual limitations of any system of shading and the need to act in an objective way when it comes to defining the limits of each class. A scheme of 4 to 6 different classes, each with its own distinctive shading and becoming heavier towards the densest population, might be the easiest to interpret visually. But, there will be situations which defy that general suggestion.

There are a number of different methods which might be used to define the density classes. The simplest would involve subdividing the range of density values into a set of classes, each having a common value. Alternatively, the classes might be determined on the basis of mean and standard deviation values derived from the actual density figures to be plotted. Working from the mean, classes might be defined in terms of plus and minus one standard deviation, plus and minus two standard deviations, and so on. Other mathematical approaches might involve using the median, upper quartile and lower quartile values to define four classes; or adopting a geometric progression, as has been used in Figure 1.2a on page 9, and conveniently incorporating the mean value of 320 persons per km.^{2} Another rather different approach would be to subdivide the range of density values into natural divisions. This involves plotting the density figures on a dispersion diagram, looking for breaks in the continuity of values, and then defining the classes in terms of these breaks.

These are but a few of a whole range of different strategies that might be followed in defining the classes chosen for choropleth maps. Inevitably, it will be asked, 'Which is best?' There is much to be said in favour of using the *natural-break* approach, but the geometric progression is valuable where the range of values is particularly wide. Equally, however, there is a strong case for the apparent objectivity offered by the mathematical approaches, such as the standard deviation and quartile methods.

There is one other issue that needs to be mentioned here. Population density per unit area is a very crude measure and there are other bases for working out population densities, such as the number of people per unit of habitable space. For example, a mean population density figure of 321 persons per km^2 for the whole of Japan grossly understates the current true density of population in that less than one-third of the country is capable of human habitation. In fact population density in the settled areas of Japan averages out at not much less than 1000 persons per km^2. Alternatively, population numbers expressed per unit of agricultural land may be a more appropriate measure in any rural area; whilst in an urban environment persons per room or dwellings per unit area might be more effective measures.

The Lorenz curve

There are other ways of analysing and depicting the distribution of population. One of these is the *Lorenz curve*. This is a graphical method widely used for analysing the spatial distribution of population in terms of its concentration and dispersion. The drawing of a Lorenz curve proceeds as follows. Mean population densities are calculated for all the equivalent units, such as wards, parishes or counties, that make up the study area. Those areal units are then ranked according to their density values. Having set out the rank order and having defined the density classes to be imposed on that rank order, the percentage of the total population and the percentage of the total area

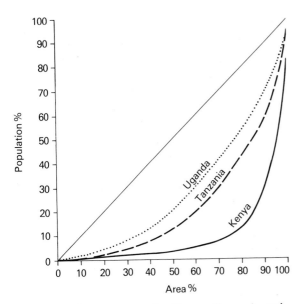

Figure 1.4 *Lorenz curves for Kenya, Tanzania and Uganda*

ASSIGNMENT

7 Compare the relative merits of the four cartographic methods used in Fig. 1.3. Then, using
the data in Table 1.1, draw four choropleth maps
showing the distribution of population in Europe:
  a. using five shadings based on a geometric
     scale
  b. using the mean and standard deviation values
     to define four shadings
  c. using an appropriate number of shadings
     based on 'natural breaks' in the range of
     values
  d. using median and quartile values to define four
     shadings.
  Finally, compare your maps with Figure 1.6
  (p. 17). Which method provides the best
  analysis of the population distribution? Why?

accounted for by all the units falling in each
density class are then calculated. The two
values derived for each density class thus allow
its position to be plotted on a graph (Fig. 1.4).
So working from the lowest density class to the
highest, the plotting enables the Lorenz curve
to be drawn. If the population were evenly
distributed, the Lorenz curve would be a
straight diagonal line across the graph.
However, the more the population is concentrated in a particular area, the more the Lorenz
curve will deviate from that line. Of the three
countries plotted on Figure 1.4, the Lorenz
curves show that Kenya has the most uneven
distribution of population, with something in
the order of 10 per cent of its population thinly
spread over about 75 per cent of its land area.
Thus 90 per cent of the people are concentrated
in the remaining 25 per cent. In contrast,
Uganda has only about 50 per cent of its population confined to 25 per cent of its territory.

Table 1.1 *The population of Europe, by country (1985)*

Country	Population density (persons per km²)
Albania	103
Austria	90
Belgium	319
Bulgaria	81
Czechoslovakia	121
Denmark	119
East Germany	154
Eire	51
Finland	15
France	101
Greece	75
Hungary	114
Iceland	2
Italy	189
Luxembourg	140
Netherlands	354
Norway	13
Poland	119
Portugal	111
Romania	95
Spain	76
Sweden	19
Switzerland	159
West Germany	245
United Kingdom	231
Yugoslavia	90
Mean	100
Standard deviation	64

POPULATION DISTRIBUTION AT DIFFERENT SPATIAL SCALES

A global view

The most crucial fact of population geography is that people are not evenly distributed across the face of the earth. This may be observed at a range of different spatial scales, from global to local. In 1985 there was an estimated 4837 million people occupying the world's land area of 150 million km^2, giving a mean population density figure of 32 persons per km^2. These figures take Antarctica into account; if it is omitted, then the mean global density is raised to 36 persons per km^2. Table 1.2 quickly reveals how much the individual continents deviate from that global mean. Asia and Europe (excluding the USSR) show mean densities just over three times the world average. At the other extreme, Oceania has a mean density less than one-tenth of the global figure, and Antarctica is virtually uninhabited. This fundamental point is driven further home by the values contained in the last two columns of Table 1.2. Asia has less than 20 per cent of the world's land surface accommodating nearly 60 per cent of the world's population. Europe is slightly less impressive with 10 per cent of the

global population concentrated on only 3 per cent of the land surface. Seemingly enjoying a favourable relationship of those two measures, Africa accounts for just over 10 per cent of the global population and 10 per cent of the land area. It is also interesting to note the strong similarity of the figures for the Soviet Union and North America.

At the macro-scale, population distribution may also be analysed in terms other than the percentage share in each continent. For example, the major concentrations of population are located towards the continental margins, whilst the interiors are characteristically sparsely populated. About 65 per cent of the world's population lives within 500 km of the coast, and 75 per cent within 1000 km. This littoral characteristic of the distribution pattern is perhaps supported by the analysis of world population in terms of its location at different altitudes. A 1960 analysis showed that 56 per cent of the population then lived between sea-level and 200 metres above, and that the mean population density within that altitudinal range was nearly twice the global average. High altitude certainly imposes limits on human habitation; the critical limit to permanent settlement varies between 5200 and 6700 metres, depending on latitude.

Less than 10 per cent of the world's popu-

	Area (km^2)	Population (millions)	Density (persons/km^2)	World land area (%)	World population (%)
Africa	30.3	555	18.3	20.2	11.5
Asia	27.6	2818	102.1	18.4	58.2
Latin America	20.6	405	19.7	13.7	8.4
North America	21.5	264	12.3	14.3	5.4
Europe (excl. USSR)	4.9	492	100.4	3.3	10.2
USSR	22.4	279	12.5	14.9	5.8
Oceania	8.5	24	2.9	5.9	0.5
Antarctica	14.0	0	0.0	9.3	0.0
World	149.8	4837	32.2	100.0	100.0
more-developed region	55.4	1180	21.3	37.0	24.4
less-developed region	94.4	3657	38.7	63.0	75.6

Table 1.2 *World population, by continent and region (1985)*

lation lives in the southern hemisphere, which is not surprising bearing in mind the relatively small amount of land therein. A similar proportion (a little less than 10 per cent of total world population) is recorded between the Equator and 10 degrees north. Nearly 50 per cent of the world's population is to be found between 20 and 40 degrees north, and 30 per cent between 40 and 60 degrees north. In total, some 80 per cent of the world's population lives within this 40 degree latitudinal band. Latitude would, therefore, appear to be a significant influence on population distribution; it does so principally through the medium of climate. In general, it is the humid and the tropical and temperate areas that offer the most conducive climates.

The Old World, comprising Europe, the USSR, and Asia, accounts for nearly 75 per cent of the world's population. The New World's percentage share, despite colonisation and development, has increased only modestly from 15 per cent to 25 per cent over the last 200 years. This particular subdivision of the globe does not coincide at all closely with the distinction that is frequently drawn today between the so-called advanced or more-developed countries and the less-developed or developing countries of the Third World. In this classification, Asia is for the most part included in the latter category. Looking at Table 1.2, the relationship between the two variables of percentage share of land surface and percentage share of total population is markedly less favourable in the case of the less-developed regions of the world; 75 per cent of the world's people are to found on 63 per cent of the land surface. Indeed, it is this mismatch that underlies the problems to be examined in Chapters 6 and 7.

Narrowing the spatial focus

The mean density figures shown in Table 1.2

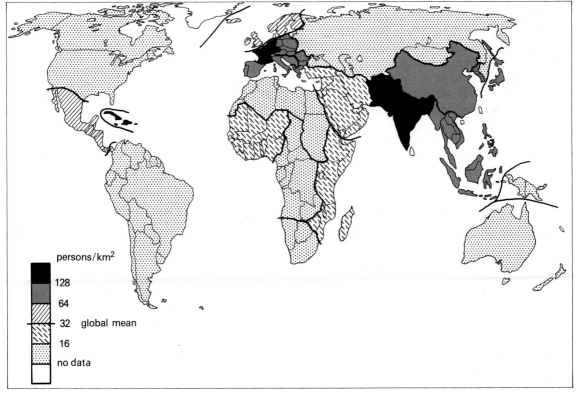

Figure 1.5 *The global distribution of population, by region (1985)*

are gross oversimplifications. In all continents there are major spatial variations in population densities. We become aware of this when we reduce the spatial scale and divide the continents into their constituent *macro-regions* and these, in turn, into their countries. For example, Figure 1.5 shows that there are regional differences within Africa, Latin America and Europe. The contrasts are particularly marked in Europe, and such contrasts remain in evidence when we narrow the spatial focus to national divisions (Fig. 1.6). The mean population densities of European countries range widely on either side of the continental average of 100 persons per km^2, from only two persons per km^2 in the case of Iceland to 354 persons per km^2 for the Netherlands. These national variations in population densities within the continent of Europe relate to such factors as the degree of urbanisation and industrial development, the richness of the resource base, altitude, climate and the general incidence of land suitable for settlement.

Figure 1.2 (p. 9) serves to build on this point by illustrating once more the two general principles that emerged when discussing the choropleth mapping technique. First, whenever population distribution is analysed in terms of spatial variations in mean density figures, there will be a degree of in-built generalisation. This masks the true character of the population distribution, no matter what the scale of the areal unit. Secondly, the larger the area used in the analysis of population distribution, the greater is the degree of generalisation embodied in the mean density figure. In Figure 1.2a, the scale of investigation has narrowed from Europe to England and Wales; analysis at a county level reveals notable variation in population densities. Those counties with large urban populations show the highest density figures. The same urban-rural differential underlies the variations in population density when we look closely at any individual county (Fig. 1.2b).

In the case of Hampshire, by no means an extreme example, the coastal urban development that relates to the cities of Southampton and Portsmouth contrasts with the relatively sparsely-populated rural areas of the New Forest and the Chalk downlands further inland (Fig. 1.2b). But even within the cities, there are important variations in population densities. In central areas, residential populations have been displaced by the expansion of commercial and other land uses. In the densely-occupied inner suburbs, housing is tightly packed and former single-family dwellings have been converted to multi-family use (Fig. 1.2c). In the less congested outer suburbs, housing is rather more spacious. Only at this *micro-scale* does one begin to appreciate the detailed nature of the actual population distribution and to realise how complex the population pattern so frequently is. It is these often important local variations in population density – some subtle, others quite striking – that are progressively lost from view as the focus of spatial analysis is gradually widened from ward to parish, from parish to county, and so on up to the continental scale.

ASSIGNMENT

---

8 With reference to the last two columns of Table 1.2:
   a. draw a diagram (or diagrams) which you think best portrays the data
   b. justify your choice, stating which continent you think shows the best combination of percentage values
   c. discuss the reasons why these two variables provide a poor basis for judging which continents might have the most serious population problems.

POPULATION DISTRIBUTION – OPPORTUNITIES AND CONSTRAINTS

The number of people in a given area, and their distribution within it, are the result of a complex interaction of factors. We should think

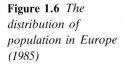

Figure 1.6 *The distribution of population in Europe (1985)*

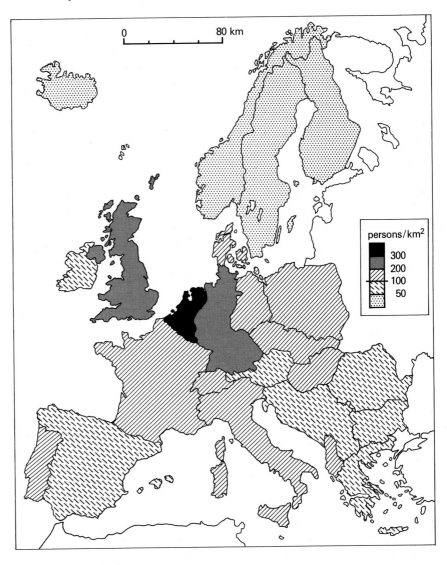

of present population as the cumulative product of population trends established over long periods of time. Whilst there is a tendency to refer to all population changes over time as *population growth*, it is important to realise that such trends can also be of either stagnation or decline. Population change is not always synonymous with population growth. As will be explained in Chapter 2, population numbers and population change are also a function of the interaction of fertility, mortality and migration. In their turn, these are conditioned by interrelated groups of factors: physical, biological, economic, social, technological and political (Fig. 1.7).

Figure 1.7 and Table 1.3 both show these factors (physical, biological, economic, etc.) which influence population distribution. These factors operate in three different ways. First, they have an indirect effect via population change. For example, social and political factors may affect fertility rates, and physical factors may affect rates of mortality (see Chapter 2). Secondly, these factors exert an influence through the medium of the *carrying capacity* of land. This is the ability of land to sustain the survival of people. This can be directly by means of food production, and indirectly through trade, whereby resources, products and services are exchanged for food. Because this capacity varies from place to place, it can be expected to play a significant part in moulding the pattern of population distribution. Table 1.3 gives some examples of the ways in which different factors may condition the carrying capacity. Thirdly, these factors

Factors	POPULATION CHANGE	CARRYING CAPACITY	POPULATION DISTRIBUTION
PHYSICAL	Natural disasters and hazards	Physical potential for food production	Limiting effects of physical extremes
	Unreliability of physical environment	Availability of natural resources	Attraction of physical optima
BIOLOGICAL	Age and sex structure	Incidence of pests reducing agricultural productivity	Contagious diseases and epidemics
	Changes in morbidity	Richness of native flora and fauna	Human physiology
ECONOMIC	Improving living standards	Degree of economic development	Location of economic activities
	Investment in medical and welfare services	Investment in resource exploitation	Productivity of agriculture
SOCIAL	Attitudes concerning children, family structure, etc.	Willingness to adopt new technology	Spatial diffusion of urbanism
	Disposition to migrate in search of better opportunities	Life styles	Ethnic identity and segregation
POLITICAL	Government promotion of family planning	Government support of the economy	Political stability and security
	Oppression, inducing migration	Regional aid programmes	Colonialism
TECHNOLOGICAL	Increasingly effective disease and death control	Introduction of improved methods of food production	Improved accessibility of remote areas
	Greater personal mobility	Ability to exploit previously marginal resources	Ability to cope with difficult environments
HISTORICAL	Evolutionary cycles of occupation	Persistence of the traditional economy	Age of peopling
	Traditional seasonal migrations	Immigrant skills	Persistence of relict patterns

Table 1.3 *The nature of selected factors affecting population change, carrying capacity and population distribution*

Figure 1.7 *Factors affecting the distribution of population*

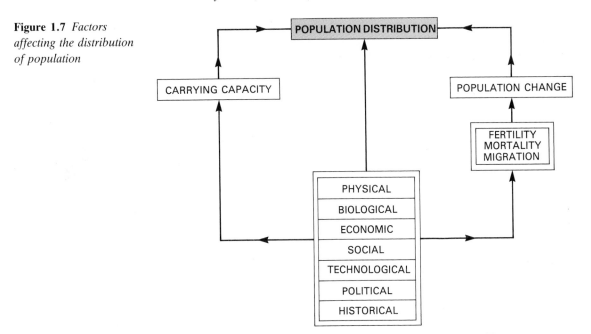

exercise a direct influence on the distribution of population, and it is this impact which is now analysed.

The influence of the physical environment

There is no doubt that those factors which fall under the general heading of *physical* have played, and continue to play, a significant role. Without being too deterministic, the physical environment does impose severe limits upon the distribution of people. The human race is a terrestrial species, so that the oceans represent vast unoccupied tracts of the world. Human physiology is also intolerant of high altitudes and of the excessively low temperatures that mark the polar parts of the world. Nevertheless, it would be wrong to think of the physical environment as acting only as a deterrent. If we look at the nature of the relationship between the physical environment and population distribution, we see that certain aspects of the environment can operate simultaneously in two different ways. Whilst the environment can act negatively as a constraint, equally it can act positively on population distribution by providing attractive opportunities. Thus, if we

look at the impact of climate on the global distribution of population, we see that population has been repelled by climatic extremes, but drawn to areas of climatic optima. Similarly, rivers may attract settlement because of the potential water supply and transport medium; on the other hand, their unpredictability in terms of flooding, the prevalence of water-borne disease, or difficulties of crossing, can lead to their having a discouraging effect upon population (Fig. 1.8).

The example of rivers makes the point that it is easy to lapse into dangerous and deterministic over-generalisations about the relationship between different environments and the distribution of population. Another example might serve to drive home this vital point. It is widely thought that highlands are sparsely populated because of their ruggedness, inaccessibility, exposure and restricted opportunities for farming. Lowlands, however, are often thought to attract dense populations through their shelter, alluvial soils and ease of movement. There are many examples to support these broad contentions; possibly none better than Japan where over 120 million people are largely confined to the fragmented lowlands which ac-

19

Figure 1.8 *A flooded main street in Dhaka, Bangladesh*
Pressure of population in Bangladesh is so great that much settlement has taken place on low-lying areas vulnerable to regular and often devastating flooding. The frequent loss of life, damage to property and widespread disruption caused by this environmental hazard are accepted as the price to be paid for living space in an overpopulated country.

Figure 1.9 *The port city of Kobe, Japan*
With only a small part of its total land surface suitable for settlement, Japan's huge urban population of over 90 million people is mainly concentrated on those discontinuous lowlands squeezed between the mountains and the sea. Intense utilisation of these coastal plains is evidenced by the carpet of tightly-packed buildings and population densities well in excess of 7000 people per km^2.

count for about a quarter of the country (Fig. 1.9). But there are also many exceptions to this theory. The existence of quite densely-settled areas in the Alps and in the Andes clearly tends to refute the generalisation about mountainous areas (Fig. 1.10). More chastening is the realisation that some of the world's most extensive lowlands and plains are amongst its most sparsely inhabited areas; for example, the Amazon and Congo lowlands, and the vast plains of the Sahara, Siberia and central Australia. Of course, these exceptional cases identify the existence and influence of other environmental factors on the populations of those areas, most notably that of climate. Climate can impinge on people in three different ways: *directly*, since some climates are more comfortable to live in, whilst others make stressful demands on human physiology; *indirectly*, through its influence on soils and vegetation, and *interactively*, as one of the factors which in combination with others condition the carrying capacity of the land (Fig. 1.7).

This view of population distribution as a response to opportunities and constraints may be applied to other aspects of the physical environment. Geology exerts at least a twofold influence. First, it conditions the nature and distribution of some sources of energy and mineral resources. Of the energy sources, coal has exerted a much greater influence on the location of industrial development, and therefore on population, than oil or natural gas (Fig. 1.11). Of the non-energy mineral resources, iron ore has, perhaps, had the greatest effect.

Figure 1.10 *An Alpine tourist resort in Canton Valais, Switzerland*
Increased leisure and affluence, together with the great popularity of winter sports, have given rise to an expanding tourist industry. Jobs, better services and improved access are a few of the benefits brought by tourism. These, in turn, have brought new life and people to many small rural settlements which, for centuries, have struggled to survive in the harsh mountain environment. Today, quite high population densities can be sustained.

Figure 1.11 *The old coal-mining settlement of Abercynon, South Wales*
The exploitation of coal resource during the 19th and early 20th centuries attracted many people to move into the South Wales coalfield. The physical geography of the area had a profound influence on the resulting settlement morphology, causing once separate colliery settlements strung out along the sheltered valleys to gradually merge into ribbons of continuous urban development.

But that effect has not always been consistent; contrast the considerable population densities associated with the ore-fields of Lorraine with the limited impact of the iron ore deposits in Venezuela, Sierra Leone or Australia. Secondly, geology exerts an interactive effect upon soils in conjunction with climate and vegetation. The significance of soils in terms of population distribution is evidenced by the very dense concentrations of populations associated with the fertile, alluvial soils of great river systems (such as the Ganges and Nile) or with the very adaptable brown earth soils. On the other hand, the persistence of highly-leached soils, such as the podsols, and the aggravation of soil erosion might be viewed as constraining aspects of soils on population patterns.

Biologically, disease may be seen as a restricting influence on population distribution in two ways. It can reduce the number of people surviving in an area by both raising levels of mortality and persuading people to remove themselves (albeit temporarily) from areas smitten by epidemics of highly-contagious diseases. The nature and incidence of disease varies from place to place. Because high temperatures accelerate biological activity, parasitic, viral and bacterial disorders are more widespread and severe in equatorial and tropical areas than in the temperate latitudes. There seems to be a fairly close correlation between the incidence of certain diseases and particular climatic environments. Yellow fever and malaria occur mainly in the inter-tropical areas of Africa and South East Asia. Tuberculosis had its origins in the towns and cities of the temperate world, but is now more widely spread in other areas as urbanisation has created extensive overcrowding and insanitary housing (Fig. 1.12). Just as diseases themselves may diffuse spatially and prompt changes in the distribution of population, so the development of modern medicine, particularly the implementation of vaccination programmes at an international scale, has generally lessened the constraining influence of disease in the world today.

Net balance and human progress

So far we have tended to see those factors affecting population distribution as black and white, as either encouraging or limiting popu-

Figure 1.12 *Riverside shanty housing in India*
The lack of proper water supply and sanitation, the crowded shack dwellings, acute poverty and proximity to a disease-ridden river are important factors contributing to the prevalence of high levels of morbidity and mortality amongst the people living in this belt of shanty housing.

lation. Yet with each and every factor there are also shades of grey; each factor can exert varying degrees of positive or negative influence, depending upon place and time. But there is one other less obvious aspect of this dual view of factors which might usefully be explored. This is the notion of *net balance*. In any area there will be a complex interaction of factors. Some of those factors will offer opportunity and others will present constraint. What is the nature of the overall balance between these two sets of factors? Does the area present rather more opportunities than contraints, or vice versa? Or rather, does the interactive effect of the opportunities outweigh the interactive effect of the constraints, or vice versa? It may be reasoned that the more the balance tips in favour of opportunities, the greater is the expectation of higher levels of population. Conversely, sparsely populated areas are probably those where constraints are likely to be very effective at the aggregate level. Possibly this is a very crude mechanism by which to explain spatial variations in the density of population. Its chief merit is that it sees population distribution as being a net response to a complicated interrelationship of factors. Some of those factors work in conjunction with one another and in the same general direction, be it encouraging or discouraging. Others operate in opposition, perhaps even to the extent of cancelling each other out.

The net balance shown in Figure 1.13 may also be viewed temporally, in that the net balance between constraints and opportunities is likely to change over time. An increase in the relative weighting of opportunities for any area may be reflected in increasing numbers of people and therefore in rising levels of population density. But what might cause the net balance to alter? Figure 1.13 shows those factors which mark the general progress of society: technological advancement, rising economic wealth and increasing government intervention. The impact of more advanced technology may alter the impact of the physical environment. Research might lead to the development of new crop species better adjusted to poor soils and climatic extremes, thereby increasing the opportunities to raise agricultural output and to support a larger population in marginal areas. Or the introduction of new mining techniques may permit the profitable working of mineral deposits previously regarded as being uneconomic by virtue of exploitation difficulties, thereby turning mere resources into workable reserves. Advances in technology can also make the unthinkable become possible.

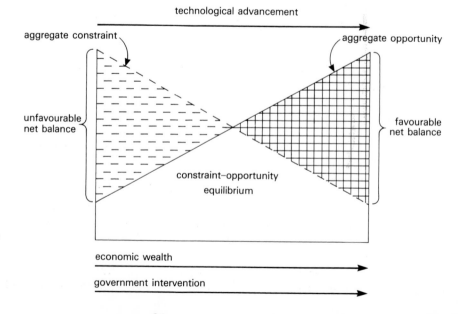

Figure 1.13 *The impact of progress on constraints and opportunities*

Figure 1.14 *A North Sea oil rig*
Market demands and technological progress have made it possible to exploit the resources of an environment distinctly hostile to human settlement and development.

Fifty years ago, who would have thought that Britain would now be deriving the bulk of its oil supply from the North Sea (Fig. 1.14)?

Not unrelated to technological progress is the theme of economic development (Fig. 1.13). As the general wealth of a society increases, so do its expectations and its willingness to invest in those areas that are able to meet its needs. The increasing leisure demands of modern affluent society, instanced by the popularity of winter sports, has meant greater exploitation of mountainous areas. Here, development was previously constrained by the lower level of demand and, in some cases, by inaccessibility and poor transport facilities. The opening up of such areas in the alpine regions of Austria, France and Switzerland has involved the construction and operation of hotels and the creation of an entire tourist infrastructure; this has all led to the creation of jobs and to the influx of both workers and visitors (Fig. 1.10, p. 21). Such developments change not only the distribution of population, but also, possibly, the type of people living there.

Increasing government intervention in both economy and society may lead to changes in the distribution of population (Fig. 1.13). Perhaps concerned by the unevenness of population distribution and economic development, governments may be prepared to offer incentives for people and firms to move from densely to sparsely populated areas. Government intervention, in a sense, alters the net balance by artificially enlarging the opportunities and reducing the constraints. Examples of this type of intervention are the planned settlement of inhospitable, but strategically important, areas of Siberia by the Soviet Government; Japan's development programmes aimed at opening up its rather unwelcoming, northernmost island of Hokkaido; and the *kibbutzim* established in the desert areas of southern Israel (Fig. 1.15).

This discussion of opportunities and constraints and their changing net balance has enabled us to identify two further groups of factors (technological and political) shown in Figure 1.7 (p. 19) as influencing the distribution of population. That leaves one further group as yet unmentioned, namely historical factors.

The imprint of the past

It would be wrong to think that the present population pattern can be wholly explained in terms of present factors; there is always going to be a relict element hanging over from the past. This relict element can persist to varying degrees over a range of different time scales. Thus the pattern of population distribution in much of Africa today closely mirrors that pattern of nineteenth-century colonisation instigated by Europeans who developed the networks of ports, mining towns and administrative centres. Similarly, the distributions of population in European industrialised countries still show concentrations of people in coalfield areas which are no longer as significant in terms of industrial development as they were during the first half of the twentieth century (Fig. 1.11, p. 22). In both cases the inherited distribution pattern is slowly being modified.

Adjustments to changing circumstances can be much quicker and comprehensive. Natural disasters, such as volcanic eruptions, earthquakes and floods, often produce immediate and quite profound consequences (Fig. 1.16). So, too, do certain types of political and military action, such as the sudden expulsion of

Figure 1.15 *The kibbutz at Jotvata, Israel*
The Israeli Government has been responsible for building many such pioneering settlements, particularly in desert areas. They have been undertaken partly to bring the desert into agricultural use, partly to provide much-needed living space for an increasing population and partly for reasons of security and territorial control.

Figure 1.16 *Devastation caused by the Armenian earthquake, December 1988*
In a matter of minutes, whole towns and cities were reduced to piles of rubble by violent earth tremors.
Fatalities in the order of tens of thousands and the mass evacuation of survivors (because of unsafe
buildings, fears of further tremors and the risk of epidemics) quickly transformed settlements like Leninakan
into ghost towns.

Asians from Uganda by the Amin regime in 1972. At the end of the Second World War, in 1945, the surrender of German territory to Poland led to the evacuation of German people, who were replaced by a smaller number of Polish settlers. This resulted in both a reduction in the overall density of population and a marked change in the pattern of distribution. Peasant settlers took over large estates which had once been the exclusive residences of aristocratic and wealthy families.

In other instances, past circumstances provide an explanation for the presence of large numbers of people in distinctly inhospitable desert and mountain environments. In the harsh Kabylie Mountains of Algeria, for example, population densities are as high as 250 persons per km^2, whilst the national average figure is 40 persons per km^2. These relatively high population densities are explained by the fact that this part of the Atlas Mountains has served as a

refuge, first for the sedentary Berbers fleeing from the invading Arabs during the seventh century, and then, much later, by the Algerians during the 1830s when the French occupied the northern plains. There are many other examples of people escaping from persecution or massacre, or being unwilling to submit to some new culture or political regime. These people have often sought refuge in inaccessible and hostile places. Such historic factors help to explain the curious inverse relationship that can exist between population density and environmental opportunities. But not all movements triggered by oppression conform in this way. The many Jews who left Germany during the Nazi persecution, before and during the Second World War, found sanctuary in the densely-populated urban areas of countries, such as the UK and the USA. Perhaps it is a little ironic that the postwar creation of the State of Israel, as a homeland for the Jews, should involve a largely difficult physical environment set in a political context of distinctly hostile, neighbouring Arab states (Fig. 1.15, p. 26).

Finally, there is the significance attached to the duration of human occupation. This adds to the impact of the past in a rather different way. In many places where people have lived in the same area for a long time, population has just grown. There is a sort of *demographic multiplier effect*. In India, where environmental conditions are hardly favourable to large populations, the national total has grown steadily over time. Thus certain areas appear today as densely-populated simply because of this process of slow demographic accumulation. As such, the process represents a very direct and persistent form of *inertia*.

ASSIGNMENTS

9 Using Table 1.3, explain the ways in which social attitudes can influence:
   a. population change
   b. carrying capacity
   c. population distribution.
10 With reference to Figure 1.12, ascertain the types of disease likely to be prevalent in shanty areas.
11 With reference to Figures 1.10 and 1.15, compare mountain and desert environments in terms of their net balances of opportunities and constraints.
12 With reference to Figures 1.8 and 1.16, compare flooding and earthquakes as environmental hazards.

CONCLUSION

The distribution of population over the earth's surface is constantly changing. The pattern today, although bearing the imprint of the past, is significantly different from what it was 100 years ago. Equally, there is every expectation that the global pattern of population distribution will be markedly different by the end of the twenty-first century. But whilst the continuing and alarming rise in the world's population (see Chapters 3 and 7) leads to a general thickening of population densities, there are some areas of the world where densities are becoming less. In a few cases it is because of declining rates of natural increase; in most others it is due to increasing mobility and people moving away. Most noteworthy here is the massive loss of population from rural areas in those countries undergoing rapid urbanisation; here many people are eagerly seeking the perceived, yet largely mythical, economic opportunities offered by the rising towns and cities. Possibly less spectacular, but of no less significance, has been the general drift of people from hostile environments. Here the impact of technological progress has made people aware that there exists a more secure and comfortable way of life not very far away.

Thus it is that the distribution of population responds to the pattern of opportunity. That pattern is conditioned by a complex interaction of many factors; by the physical environment, by the economic development of that environment and by the reappraisal of that environment in the light of such things as technological progress, military need or political expediency. But at all times, the pattern of the past distribution tends to act as a skeleton, haunting the present pattern.

ASSIGNMENTS

13 Obtain population data from the most recent census for your local area (region or county) and map the distribution of population. Identify the factors which appear to influence the present pattern, and try to assess the relative importance of those factors.
14 For the same area, obtain population data from a census taken 50 years or more ago. Again map the data. Compare this map with the one you have already produced showing the present distribution. In what ways has the population pattern changed? How might you explain those changes?

2

Fertility, Mortality and Natural Change

COMPONENTS OF POPULATION CHANGE

The previous chapter made the point that the main concern of population geography is the spatial distribution of population. It is perhaps tempting to think that spatial distribution is something which is static and unchanging. This is far from true, for the distribution pattern is, most often, highly dynamic. It constantly changes, not just because the overall population may be either increasing or decreasing, but also because gains and losses of population are being experienced at the same time in different parts of the pattern.

Figure 2.1 shows that population change, be it *positive* (growth) or *negative* (decline), has two main components. The population of an area will experience *natural increase* when the number of births exceeds the number of deaths; conversely, population will experience *natural*

decrease when deaths outnumber births. This component of population change is known as *natural change* or *reproductive change*. The other component, *migrational change*, will lead to population increase when the number of people entering an area exceeds the number leaving. On the other hand, where departures exceed arrivals, there will be a net loss of people. Thus it can be seen that the total population of an area, and the trends in total population over time, are the outcome of the interaction of these two components of change. There is always a sort of *dynamic equilibrium* between them. The size of the population at any one time may be likened to the level of water in a tank which is filled by two pipes (births and inward migration) and emptied by two drains (deaths and outward migration) (Fig. 2.1).

The subject of migration will be explored in Chapter 4, but for the moment it is helpful to sow the seed of a basic idea. The relative importance of natural and migrational change varies considerably from place to place and from time to time. In broad terms, the two components can assume two different combinations, producing three different outcomes. They can work together, either increasing or decreasing the population of an area; or they can work against each other (Fig. 2.2). When working against each other the impact of the one is, to varying degrees, cancelled by the impact of the other. The outcome is, therefore, a reduction in the potential scale of population change.

In this chapter discussion is confined to one of these two components of population change – natural change. We shall first examine separately the two key influences of fertility and mortality, and then look at their changing relationships.

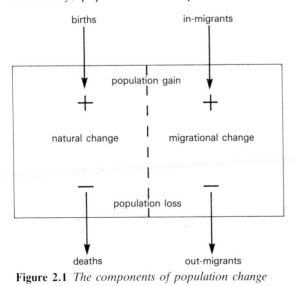

Figure 2.1 *The components of population change*

Figure 2.2 *The outcomes of four different combinations of the population change components*

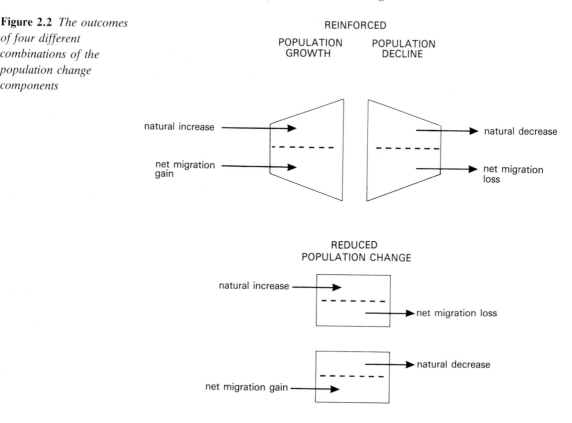

FERTILITY – DEFINITION AND MEASUREMENT

As is common in many fields of study, it is necessary at the outset to define what we mean by certain terms. In particular we need to distinguish between *fertility, fecundity* and *reproduction*. These are three words which are commonly used rather loosely and interchangeably, thereby implying, quite wrongly, that they mean the same thing. In common usage, *fertility* refers to the ability of living things to bear offspring and to produce – be it food, ideas or whatever. In population studies, however, whilst fertility broadly indicates the creative element in natural change, as distinct from the destructive element of death, it specifically means the actual occurrence of *live-births*. In this sense therefore, fertility is not to be confused with *fecundity*. This refers to the , capacity of people to bear children and thereby perpetuate themselves; it really relates to the absence of sterility. But fertility and fecundity are quite different from *reproduction*. In population studies reproduction means the degree to which people, within a given age range, are replaced by people of the same age a generation later. Hence, the *net reproduction rate* shows the relative size of a generation in relation to the generation that preceded it.

Just as the definition of fertility poses its problems, so does its measurement. First, there is the irrefutable fact that, whilst the vital registration of births is widely practised throughout the world, data on births tend to be both incomplete and inaccurate. The wish to conceal illegitimacy, the suppression of female births (which still persists in certain areas today) and the failure to distinguish between *live-* and *still-births* mean that our assessments of fertility, based on available birth data, inevitably have their margins of error in many parts of the world.

The simplest measure of fertility is provided by the *crude birth rate*. This is the ratio between the number of live-births during a given period (normally one year) and the total population of the country or region (normally the mid-year total). It is expressed as births per thousand people. National crude birth rates in the world today mostly fall within the range 15–50 per 1000. But, as the name suggests, the assessment of fertility is a crude one, and its limitations become quite serious when it comes to comparing fertility levels in different countries or regions. The chief drawback is that the crude birth rate does not take into account the *age* and *sex structure* of the population. For example, it is possible for the same crude birth rate to be derived from two very different demographic situations. Region A has a high proportion of elderly people, but a moderate level of fertility is maintained because those people in the reproductive age range happen to be quite prolific. In contrast, Region B has a younger population, but the crude birth rate is the same because widespread practice of birth control has lowered the level of fertility. In terms of potential population growth, however, there could be a considerable difference between the two regions, with the younger population of B offering greater fecundity and therefore a potentially higher rate of natural increase.

But, for all its shortcomings as regards the assessment of future prospects, the crude birth rate is nonetheless an important and widely-used demographic measure. It is easy to compute. It is easily understood by those with little demographic knowledge, and it can be quite effective in detecting both general differences and changes in population growth. Also, it can be calculated or estimated for those parts of the world where the general dearth of demographic data debars the computation of more sophisticated measures of fertility.

The crude birth rate may be refined in a number of different ways. The easiest method is by expressing live-births, not in terms of total population, but as a percentage of the number of adults; or, even better, of the number of women of reproductive age (generally, but not always, taken to be between the ages of 15 and 49). The latter computation is known as the *general fertility rate*. The measure may be further refined by taking into account the age factor. This is achieved by expressing the number of births to mothers of a given age as a percentage of all the women of the same age in that population. Such *age-specific birth rates* derived for each year of reproductive age may be summed to give what is known as the *total fertility rate*. Both the general fertility rate and the total fertility rate offer reasonably reliable measures for regional and international comparisons, provided there is agreement over common criteria. For example, is it agreed by everyone that only live-births should be counted and that live-births outside marriage should be included?

Somewhat different is the *fertility ratio*. This is normally calculated by expressing the number of children under five years of age as a percentage of the number of women in the reproductive age range. The main disadvantage with this measure is that it cannot be calculated annually, but only for the five years preceding a census. Another drawback is that the ratio refers to the number of children surviving to the age of four; because of infant mortality this number will be less (in some areas quite markedly so) than the number of children who were actually born.

Finally, there is one other refined fertility measure that needs to be noted; it is referred to as the *standardised birth rate*. It is particularly useful for investigating fertility differences within a given country, as for example between regions or between urban and rural areas. The statistical procedures for deriving the standardised birth rate are somewhat laborious. In essence, they simply involve calculating the birth rate that would have occurred in a particular area if the age structure of that area's population had been the same as that of the country as a whole. By comparing this standardised birth rate with the national birth rate (usually by expressing the former as a percentage of the latter), it is possible to derive an index of relative fertility. If the percentage values are greater than 100 (i.e. the standardised birth rate is greater than the national birth rate), the area can be defined as having relatively high fertility, and vice versa.

ASSIGNMENT

---

1 Describe the different measures used to assess the fertility of a population, and assess their relative merits.

FERTILITY – PATTERNS, TRENDS AND FACTORS

Patterns

Fertility varies greatly in space and time. The first part of this statement may be verified by looking at two global maps (Figs 2.3 and 2.4). Figure 2.3 shows the crude birth rates for the major regions of the world. The values can be seen to differ quite widely from the global average of 27 live-births per 1000 people per year. By far the highest birth rates occur in West and East Africa, where the rates are over 47 per 1000. A belt of slightly lower birth rates (between 37 and 47 per 1000) extends from South to North Africa and across the Middle East; also in this category is Oceania (excluding Australia and New Zealand). Central and South America, the Caribbean and South and South East Asia constitute the third category; these regions have rates only slightly above the global mean. The Soviet Union and China form the next category down; together they account for a large part of the Eurasian land mass and interestingly share the same crude birth rate of 19 per 1000. Finally, there are the 'European' regions of the world (Europe, North America

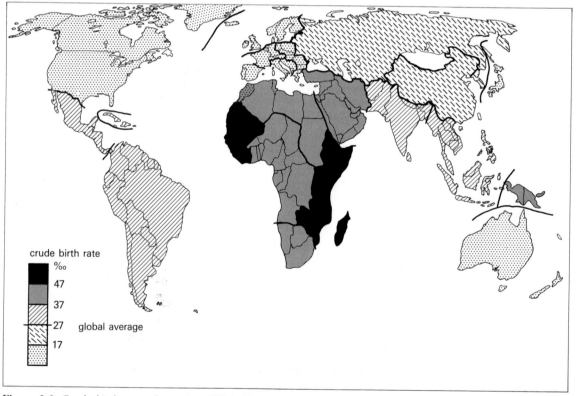

Figure 2.3 *Crude birth rates, by region (1980–85)*

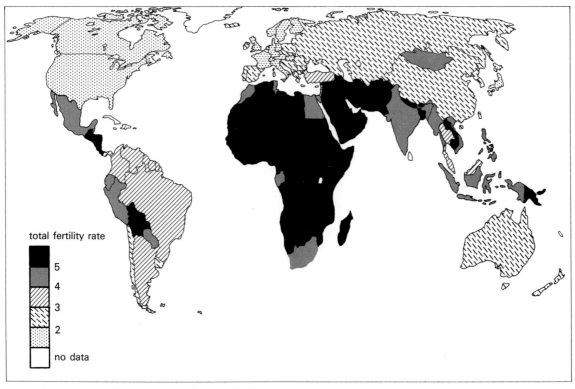

Figure 2.4 *Total fertility rates, by country (1984)*

and Australasia). These, together with Japan, show rates less than 17 per 1000.

It is important to remember that Figure 2.3 shows regional averages. Some of the regions show a degree of uniformity, in that the values of individual countries fall within the same fairly narrow range. This is certainly true of the regions showing the highest crude birth rates. In West Africa, for instance, the range is from 47 per 1000 (Guinea) to 51 per 1000 (Niger). On the other hand, there are regions which show strong international variations. For example, in the lowest category, the crude birth rate of West Germany (9.5 per 1000) is half that of Ireland; in South America, Bolivia's rate of 47 per 1000 is nearly treble that of Uruguay; whilst in the Middle East, Jordan's birth rate, 45 per 1000, is almost twice that of neighbouring Israel.

Figure 2.4 uses a different, and more accurate, measure of fertility, the *total fertility rate*. Remember, this indicates the number of chil-

dren that a woman may be expected to bear during her lifetime, given prevailing *age-specific fertility rates*. Whilst the data relate to individual countries, it is clear that the distribution pattern allows us to make some generalisations at a regional level. And at this level we may also compare Figures 2.3 and 2.4. The fertility rates range from eight in Rwanda to just over one in Denmark and West Germany. Virtually the whole of Africa and the Middle East stand out as one huge continuous area experiencing the highest rates of fertility. Scattered values in excess of five are also to be found in Central America (El Salvador, Guatemala, Honduras and Nicaragua), South America (Bolivia), South Asia (Bangladesh, Bhutan and Nepal), and in South East Asia (Laos). At the other end of the scale, North America again appears as a region of very low fertility (less than two). But Europe is divided, with much of East and South Europe falling in the next category up, along with Australia and New Zealand, the

Soviet Union and China. Of the two remaining intermediate categories, South and South East Asia generally show a fertility rate of four, and much of South America has a rate of three.

Trends

Figures 2.3 and 2.4 present a snapshot view of global fertility in the mid-1980s. It is important to stress, however, that fertility varies not only from place to place, but also from time to time. This can be readily demonstrated by simply looking at changes in crude birth rates experienced by a sample of countries over the relatively short time-span of 55 years; these changes are shown by the upper line of each

graph in Figure 2.5. In all cases the crude birth rate today is lower than it was in 1930. But the degree of decline has varied from country to country. In China and Singapore the fall has been spectacular, with rates more than halved. In other countries, notably Egypt, Israel and Japan, decline has been more gradual, but even in Japan the rate has been nearly halved. In the United Kingdom the rate has been subject only to minor fluctuations, in stark contrast to the marked oscillations experienced in Nigeria and Mauritius. Although the overall trend of these crude birth rates has been downward, there remain today considerable differences in their general level – as for example between Nigeria and Japan, Ecuador and the United Kingdom.

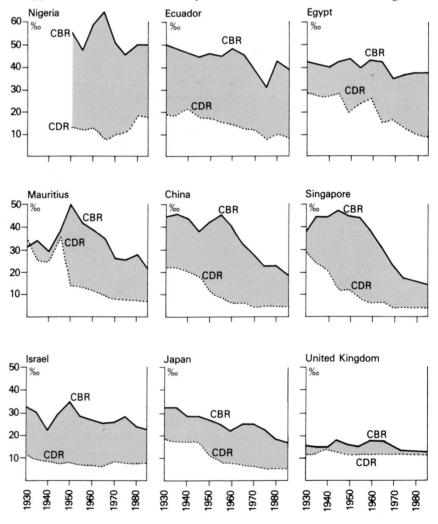

Figure 2.5 *Crude birth and death rates for selected countries (1930–1985)*

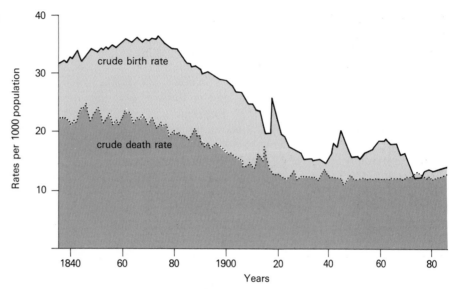

Figure 2.6 *Crude birth and death rates for England and Wales (1837–1985)*

The graph for the United Kingdom in Figure 2.5 might give the misleading impression that fertility has always been low. However, Figure 2.6 takes a longer-term view and clearly shows that fertility in England and Wales used to be very much higher. The point to be made, therefore, is basically this: the countries which are today experiencing declining fertility are simply moving along the path followed earlier by those countries in North America, Europe and Australasia, which are shown by Figure 2.3 as now having low fertility. This idea of a common pathway being followed by all countries – but at different times and rates – is explored in the next chapter.

	Jews	Moslems
	(live births per 1000)	
1936	29.7	53.1
1937	26.5	49.8
1938	26.3	47.3
1939	23.0	46.4
1940	23.7	47.4
1941	20.7	49.9
1942	22.7	45.2
1943	29.0	52.4
1944	30.2	53.7
1945	30.2	·54.2

Table 2.1 *Differential fertility rates in Palestine (1936–1945)*

Factors

Why does fertility vary in the two dimensions of time and space? The causal factors are many and diverse, but they may be broadly grouped under the following headings: demographic, economic, social, cultural, political and environmental. It would be difficult, and indeed foolish, to attempt to rank these factors according to their importance. Not only are many of these factors interrelated, but their relative influence varies in those same two dimensions.

The factor of birth control is a good case in point. It includes contraception, sterilisation, abortion and abstention. Although the level of knowledge about modern birth control methods differs in many parts of the world, particularly between developing and developed countries, this is not the complete explanation for the marked differences in the degree to which use is made of such methods. The whole status of birth control is considerably influenced by a complex of interrelated factors falling under most of those category headings just mentioned. For example, most of the great religions of the world favour fertility and the rearing of large families, and are opposed to most forms of contraception. One notable exception is Protes-

35

tantism, moulded by a Malthusian fear of over-population. The impact of different religious attitudes is well illustrated if we compare the fertility rates of Protestant and Catholic communities. In the British Isles, today's crude birth rate in largely Protestant Scotland is 13 per 1000, whilst in the Catholic Irish Republic the rate is 17.5 per 1000. Table 2.1 shows large differences in the fertility of Jews and Moslems.

It is not simply a matter of certain religions advocating larger families. In parts of Africa, the Middle East and Asia, society decrees that men should father many children, as a mark of their virility and as a status symbol (Fig. 2.7). There are also rather more pragmatic arguments. These apply particularly in those parts of the world where there is high infant mortality and low life expectancy; or where cheap labour is needed to ensure family survival. Children can also be seen as offering support for parents when they reach old age, and this can become an important consideration in those less-developed countries lacking social services for the elderly. Equally, in other parts of the world, children can be perceived as a drain on resources and an impediment to socio-economic advancement. In the circumstances, a resort to birth control is understandable. Such, surely, is the practice of most DINKYs (dual income, no kids yet)!

Birth control is nothing new. Various forms of abstinence, including delayed marriages, are deeply embedded in the practices of many traditional societies. China and Japan are among those countries where *infanticide* (the elimination of unwanted children, especially girls) was formerly practised; abortion remains a widespread practice there. But, in the twentieth century, the assault on fertility has been sustained at a higher level and over much more of the globe. This is a culmination of technological advances (new and more reliable methods of contraception, safer abortions and sterilisations), education and a growing awareness of the problems that lie in the wake of an uncontrolled growth in population. It is mainly for the last of these reasons that birth control has become an integral part of government

Figure 2.7 *A Mali mother and her children Although the mother is aged only 25, she has already borne four children and a fifth is expected. Given that she might look forward to a further 20 years of fecundity, there is a strong likelihood that, when complete, her family might be double its present number. The reasons for having such large numbers of children are complex and cannot be simply put down to an ignorance of birth control methods.*

policy. China, for example, has promoted the 'one-child family', Singapore had a 'please stop at two' policy, and India offers rewards for

晚婚晚育献身四化

(a)

Figure 2.8 *Posters promoting birth control in* **(a)** *China and* **(b)** *Nepal*
Faced with a population of over 1000 million fast outstripping the ability of the economy to support it, China has had to introduce stringent measures to persuade couples to limit their families to one child only. In Nepal, with an annual population growth rate of 2.6 per cent and per capita GNP at only $160, the target is to encourage families of no more than two children.

those of reproductive age undergoing sterilisation (Fig. 2.8). In all three countries, encouragement of birth control has been given because of a national need to achieve a better balance between population and resources (Chapter 6). But let it be emphasised that not everyone believes in birth control.

Equally, it should be pointed out that government intervention in a demographic context has not always been designed to curb fertility. In theory, Marxism is opposed to birth

(b)

गुलाफ चक्की दिनका दिन
नविर्सी खानु
हरेक दिन

गुलाफ
औषधी पसलबाट किन्नुहोस

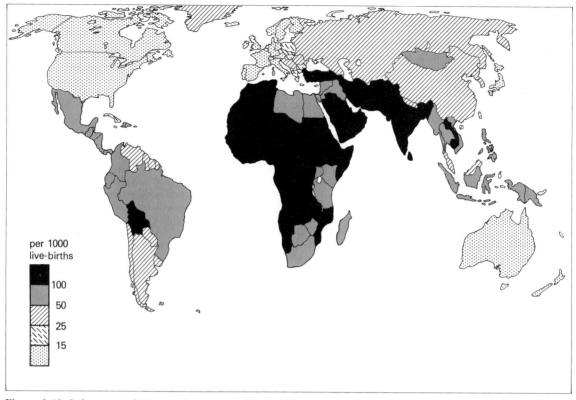

Figure 2.12 *Infant mortality rates, by country (1984)*

has occurred during the second half of this century, but this time it has been mainly experienced in the developing world. Here, a combination of economic development, aid from the advanced economies, and effective medical campaigns against infectious diseases have led to a marked decline in mortality.

Bearing in mind this two-phased 'retreat of death', let us look at the crude death rates plotted in Figure 2.5 (p. 34). It is immediately apparent that Nigeria and the United Kingdom are exceptions to the general rule. There has been a rise in mortality in the former, whilst in the latter the crude death rate was exactly the same in 1985 as it was in 1930. The remaining countries may be distinguished according to the degree of reduction in mortality experienced over the 55-year period. In Singapore and Mauritius the reduction has been by a factor of five, in China by four, and in Egypt and Japan by three. In the case of Israel (formerly Pales-

tine), mortality was low even in 1930, but nonetheless there has been a further reduction. What is also apparent is that the differences between countries are less today than they were in 1930, and that the differences are notably smaller than those between crude birth rates. Thus, we might conclude that the second phase of the 'retreat from death' has prompted *convergence* – countries in various parts of the world have become more alike. That convergence might also lend support to the idea floated earlier (and developed in the next chapter) that the course of demographic history tends to be the same the world over. All countries follow the same general pathway or model, but at different times and speeds.

One automatic consequence of the decline in mortality is the raising of life expectancy. An analysis of six European countries has shown that between 1840 and 1955 mean life expectancy increased from 41 to 71 years. Table 2.7

Figure 2.13 *Residential renewal in Singapore*
Government programmes have brought about the gradual replacement of old and obsolescent dwellings by modern apartment blocks. Much has been achieved in terms of raising the general level of residential conditions and reducing the incidence of those exogenetic causes of mortality associated with substandard housing. Even poor families now have access to accommodation which includes a kitchen, a bathroom and toilet, and is serviced by running water, piped sewerage and electricity.

45

tions, and severe tropical storms can cause an immense loss of life and therefore a sudden upswing in the mortality rate (Figs. 2.15, 1.8 p. 20 and 1.16, p. 27). Table 2.10 gives some idea of the scale of fatality associated with recent environmental disasters. The chances of reducing the impact of such events in the future are slim. The really catastrophic events are so infrequent as to deter investment in possible protective measures, whilst population pressure in particular areas will ensure that people continue to take a gamble that the unthinkable will never happen. From the environmental viewpoint, the outlook does seem to be distinctly bleak; increasing global pollution, the widening hole in the ozone layer, and the relentless exploitation of physical and biotic resources offer no prospect of a reduction in the rate of mortality attributable to environmental hazards.

1865 (per thousand deaths)		1985 (per thousand deaths)	
Infectious diseases	321	Circulatory system	479
Respiratory diseases	148	Neoplasms (cancers)	242
Nervous system	129	Respiratory diseases	108
Digestive system	83	Accidents	32
Circulatory system	53	Digestive system	31

Table 2.11 *Principal causes of death in Great Britain (1865 and 1985)*

Finally, no discussion of mortality would be complete without some reference to the causes of death. These undoubtedly vary in the two dimensions of time and space and so contribute to differential mortality rates; they also vary according to the age-group of the deceased. The causes of death fall broadly into two categories. First there are the *endogenetic* causes which are either *congenital* (such as deformities or diseases dating from birth) or *degenerative* (associated with the ageing and gradual wearing out of the body e.g. cancer, senility and circulatory disorders). Secondly there are the *exogenetic* causes which are the result of environmental conditions; indeed, they are sometimes referred to as the *environmental* causes. These include infectious,

Figure 2.15 *Hurricane damage in Miami, Florida Of all the environmental hazards, tropical storms are responsible in most years for the greatest number of fatalities. This arises because of their frequency, severity and widespread nature, and because they often strike densely-populated parts of the developing world. However, the photograph makes the point that such storms can also wreak havoc and cause death in the more-developed areas outside the tropics.*

Type of event	1960s	1970s
Drought	10 100	231 100
Flood	23 700	46 800
Tropical cyclone	107 500	343 600
Earthquake	52 500	389 700
Other hazards	28 900	129 600

Table 2.10 *Global environmental hazard fatalities, per year (1960–1979)*

Figure 2.16 *A multiple pile-up on a French road*
Unlike most exogenetic causes of death, the incidence of fatal road accidents is increasing in many parts of the world. Driver error is the common cause – excessive speed, driving without due care or under the influence of alcohol or drugs. But there are many other contributory factors, often of an environmental nature; greatly swollen volumes of road traffic, outmoded roads and climatic hazards (fog, ice and torrential rain), to name but a few.

pulmonary and digestive diseases which are linked with climate, diet, housing conditions, pollution and social habits such as smoking (cancer), drinking (alcoholism) drugs and promiscuity (AIDS), also included are deaths by accident (Fig. 2.16). Many of the infectious diseases (particularly tuberculosis) which used to be common causes of death in urban areas have been reduced or eradicated. Despite this, urban areas continue to show higher rates of *morbidity* or incidence of certain exogenetic causes, notably road accidents and those diseases associated with the pace and stress of city living. In general, the spread of modern medicine, and greater effectiveness in dealing with the control of disease, is reducing the exogenetic causes of death. An obvious consequence of this death control is that endogenetic causes, especially neoplasms (cancers), are now accounting for a large proportion of deaths (Table 2.11). Certainly, the principal causes of death in Britain today are different from those of a hundred years ago; eight out of every ten deaths are now due to endogenetic causes. One wonders to what extent the spread of AIDS will alter this situation throughout the world.

ASSIGNMENTS

10 Compare Figures 2.10, 2.11 and 2.12. Which two of these maps show the most similar patterns? Explain why this might be so.

11 Graph the data contained in Table 2.7. What have been the main factors responsible for this rise in life expectancy in Japan?

12 Do you think that the causes of rising life expectancy in Japan are the same as those prompting the increases in the developing countries shown in Figure 2.14? Justify your viewpoint.

13 Suggest possible explanations for the relationships shown in Tables 2.8 and 2.9.

NATURAL CHANGE

Measurement

In population geography, *natural change* refers to the change in population numbers resulting from alterations in the balance between births and deaths. Natural change can be either positive or negative; most often, it is the former. *Natural increase* is the difference between the number of births and the number of deaths recorded in an area over a given period, assuming that births exceed deaths. The *natural increase rate* is the difference between the crude birth and death rates during a year, again assuming that the former exceeds the latter. Whilst this is a widely-used measure of population change, like the crude birth and death rates from which it is derived, it is at best an imperfect approximation. To be at all meaningful, it is necessary to take into account the age-structure of a population, particularly the relative importance of the population falling within the reproductive age-range. To this end, demographers have produced a number of more refined measures of natural change. These include the *gross reproduction rate*, the *net reproduction rate* and the *vitality rate*.

The *gross reproduction rate* is calculated by adding up all the age-specific birth rates for women in the age-range 15 to 49, dividing by 1000, and multiplying by the proportion of births which are female. Thus it shows how many girls would be born to a newly-born girl during her lifetime, supposing that she survives to the age of 50 and that there are no changes in female fertility. If the rate equals one, then it means that one generation of females would be replaced exactly by the next. If the rate is less, then there is the prospect of natural decrease and vice versa. The *net reproduction rate* is a refinement, in that it takes into account the possibility of death before the age of 50. Thus, in the calculation, each age-specific birth rate is multiplied by the survival rate for that age. The *index of vitality* is a somewhat different measure. It is derived by multiplying the total fertility rate by the percentage of the population aged 20 to 40, and dividing that by the product of the crude death rate multiplied by the *old-age index* (the ratio of the over 60s to the under 20s). Three categories are normally recognised on the basis of the index value: over 8, 4 to 8, and under 4. There is no particular significance attached to each of these values, other than as a sequence (running from high to low values) indicating increasing degrees of youthfulness.

Patterns

The examination of fertility and mortality rates has shown that they both vary from place to place and from time to time. Equally, the relationship between these two components of population change can vary, giving rise to patterns of natural increase which are constantly changing. Figure 2.17 seeks to show the global pattern in the early 1980s. Since crude birth and death rates have been used, the map cannot be taken as giving a precise indication of the distribution of population change. Nonetheless, it does permit us to identify some broad

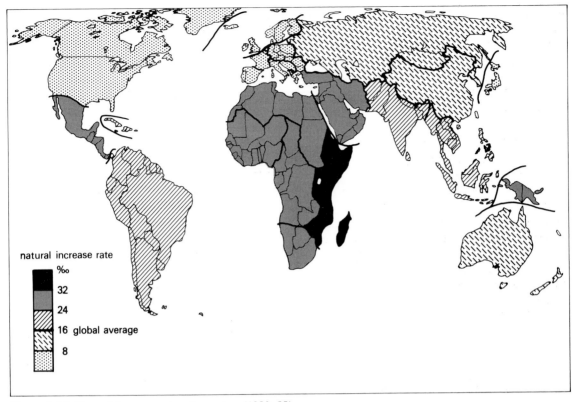

Figure 2.17 *Natural increase rates, by region (1980–85)*

features. In relation to the global average of 16 per 1000, most of Africa, the Middle East, Central America and Oceania (outside Australasia) show a rate at least 50 per cent higher, whilst in East Africa the rate is in fact double the world average. Clearly, what are being signalled here are regions of fast population growth. At the other extreme, there are North America, all of Europe and Japan showing low rates of natural increase. North and West Europe, with rates as low as 1 per 1000, would appear to be on the brink of population stagnation. Between these two extremes, South America, the Caribbean, South and South East Asia show rates slightly above the global mean, whilst the rates for the USSR, China and Australasia are slightly below. Thus the essential message of Figure 2.17 is that the developing and developed regions of the world may be broadly distinguished in terms of natural increase, falling as they do into the opposing camps of fast and slow population growth respectively. That is a significant distinction to be explored both in the next chapter and in Chapter 6.

Figure 2.5 (p. 34) establishes the basic point (also to be elaborated in the next chapter) that rates of natural increase do change considerably over relatively short periods of time. For example, rates of natural increase have increased in the developing countries of Egypt and Mauritius; in China, Israel and the United Kingdom they have declined. In other cases the situation has been one of little overall change, but with short-term, and often abrupt, fluctuations occurring during the 50-year period. Nigeria, Ecuador, Singapore and Japan would appear to fall in this last category. But clearly there is a significant difference in the level of natural increase as between the first two, which are developing countries, and the last two, which are more developed.

	Decennial percentage population increase		Percentage share of world population	
	1920–30	1970–80	1930	1980
Africa	11.3	33.3	7.7	11.2
North America	15.4	11.0	6.7	5.5
Latin America	19.6	27.5	5.5	8.3
Asia	11.0	23.6	53.3	58.4
Europe	8.2	5.4	18.6	10.3
Oceania	18.2	19.2	0.5	0.5
USSR	11.4	9.5	7.7	5.8
World	11.3	20.9	100.0	100.0

Table 2.12 *World population change, by continent (1930–1980)*

Table 2.12 illustrates the same point, but at a continental scale and using a rather different measure, the *decennial percentage increase*. This is derived using the formula:

$$\frac{Pj - Pi}{Pi} \times 100$$

where *Pi* is the population at the beginning of the 10-year period and *Pj* is the population at the end. As such, this gives some indication of the scale of population growth produced by natural increase. It will be seen that, although all regions have shown population growth (and in a majority of cases the rate has risen between the two sample decades), there are considerable regional differences. Table 2.12 also illustrates the point that, when these differences in rates of natural increase and population growth prevail for some time, they can profoundly affect the global distribution of population. In Africa, Asia and Latin America the rates of growth have been so high, and presumably have persisted throughout the 50-year period, that each has increased its percentage share of the world's total population. These regions have gained at the expense of the slower-growing regions (Europe, the USSR and North America), whose percentage shares have declined. Thus, once again, we

have demonstrated that the spatial distribution of population is a highly dynamic one.

ASSIGNMENTS

14 Compare Figures 2.3, 2.10 and 2.17.
   a. To what extent do they appear to show the same broad pattern? Summarise that pattern.
   b. Identify those regions which appear to be the exceptions to the general pattern noted.

15 Assess the relative merits of measuring population growth by the method used in Table 2.12, as compared with other measures described on p. 50.

16 Using the data in Table 2.12, draw a diagram to illustrate the changes in the global distribution of population. Write a short analytical account of those changes.

CONCLUSION

At the global scale, all population growth is the product of natural increase. The rate of natural increase is, therefore, a key influence on population change. That rate is essentially the outcome of the balance achieved in a population as between fertility and mortality, the creation and destruction of people. History shows that these two attributes, in their turn, have been susceptible to changes which reflect broader developments in human society and economy. At any given time, the balance between fertility and mortality can vary quite markedly from place to place. This is as true today as it was 100 years ago. Equally, at any given location, be it in the more- or less-developed regions of the world, that balance can fluctuate from time to time and to varying degrees. It is these two-dimensional changes in natural increase which are powerful forces moulding what, after all, is the prime focus of population geography – the spatial distribution of population.

3

The Demographic Transition

WORLD POPULATION GROWTH

This chapter is about population change – change in numbers, change in fertility and mortality rates, change in the relationship between those two variables, and, therefore, shifts in the nature and rate of natural change. The emphasis is very definitely on the time dimension. The temptation to say that this sounds like history rather than geography may be refuted on at least two grounds. First, it is important that the geographer should have some awareness of the time context. After all, most of what we observe today is, in effect, an inheritance from the past. Thus in order to make sense of the present, we need some awareness of what happened yesterday. Secondly, the nature and degree of change are two powerful measures by which geographers may distinguish between different parts of the globe. In this respect, population change is no exception, allowing us to make highly significant distinctions, particularly at an international level. It is this particular viewpoint which will be adopted throughout much of this chapter.

Leaving aside the contentious matter of when exactly it was that the species *homo sapiens* first evolved, it has been estimated that the entire population of the world today could be the offspring of six couples living no more than 100 000 years ago. This estimate assumes population growth at the very slow rate of 0.002 per cent per annum (one-hundredth of what it is today). The history of the human race is, of course, longer (probably more than 500 000 years) and it is likely that for most of that time mortality rates were high, requiring human reproduction at near-biological or maximum capacity. That high mortality (caused by famine, war and epidemics) also explains why cultures in all parts of the world have traditionally placed great emphasis on fertility. Of the major factors limiting growth in early prehistoric times, food supply was probably the most critical. Initially, it was derived by gathering and hunting, but during the Neolithic period (c. 7000 to 2000 BC), the invention and spread of agriculture greatly improved the situation. Indeed, it led to the first *population explosion*.

Given that the first national censuses were not taken until about 200 years ago, it follows that any assessment of the scale and growth of the human population before that time must be largely a matter for conjecture. The surviving evidence is both scanty and unreliable. It has been suggested that at the beginning of the Christian era, global population amounted to 300 million; and that over the next 1500 years, it less than doubled, reaching a figure of something over 500 million (Fig. 3.1). Since 1650 population growth has increased at an exponential rate. It doubled between 1650 and 1850; it doubled again between 1850 and 1950; and

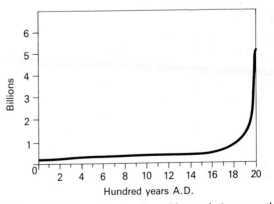
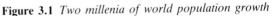

Figure 3.1 *Two millenia of world population growth*

it has almost doubled again since then. In 1987 world population passed the five billion mark. This alarming population explosion has been ignited by a series of advances which include the economic progress created by the Agricultural and Industrial Revolutions of the late eighteenth century onwards, and progress of a more social kind derived from modern science and technology. The net impact of this progress has been to reduce mortality rates and to raise fertility rates.

	(% of total population)						
	1650	1700	1750	1800	1850	1900	1950
Africa	20	16	14	10	9	8	8
Asia	57	63	64	66	62	56	55
Latin America	2	2	1	1	3	4	6
North America	<1	<1	<1	1	2	5	7
Europe (incl. USSR)	20	18	20	21	24	27	23
Oceania	<1	<1	<1	<1	<1	<1	<1
Total population (millions)	545	622	728	900	1201	1608	2510

Table 3.1 *The changing distribution of the world's population, by continent (1650–1950)*

It is appropriate that we should briefly examine the spatial distribution of this population growth over the last 300 years. The two outstanding features illustrated by Table 3.1 are the dominance of Asia, with its fluctuating share of global population rising to as high as 66 per cent in 1800, and the demise of Africa, with its percentage share falling by over one-half. As regards the latter, Africa south of the Sahara literally lost population as a result of the transportation of slaves, principally to the USA. The estimated loss of some 50 million people as a result of that trade certainly helped to depress the rate of population growth. Indeed, during the 300 years shown by Table 3.1, the population of the whole of Africa only doubled; whereas in Asia and Europe populations were multiplied by factors of four and

five respectively. Since 1950, however, the situation in Africa has changed quite dramatically (contrast Table 1.2 on p. 14 with Table 2.12 p. 52). Despite oscillating values, Europe (including the USSR) maintained its second ranking throughout the period. The impact of the Industrial Revolution is possibly reflected in the rising values between 1750 and 1900. Like Africa in the eighteenth century, Europe also shed population, as European settlers colonised the New World. Long-distance migration, therefore, has played a significant part in changing the distribution of the world's population, curbing growth rates in Africa and Europe, and at the same time enhancing growth rates in the Americas and Oceania.

ASSIGNMENTS

1. Explain how each of the following has influenced population growth:
   a. the Agricultural Revolution
   b. the Industrial Revolution
   c. medical science.
2. Show the information contained in Table 3.1 by means of appropriate cartographic techniques. Justify your choice of techniques, explaining their advantages over other possible methods.
3. With reference to Table 3.1, comment on the advantages and disadvantages of using either absolute figures or percentages in reviewing world population growth, area by area, over a period of time.

THE PROCESS OF DEMOGRAPHIC TRANSITION

Whilst the present world population expansion is due to a widening gap between fertility and mortality rates, historical analysis of trends in more advanced countries suggests that populations, in fact, undergo a process termed the *demographic transition*. Basically, the transition is the change from high to low rates of fertility and mortality. Identification and early explanation of the process can be traced to the writings of Thompson (1929) and Notestein (1945). Central to their explanation is the *theory of demographic regulation*. This states that every society tends to keep the vital processes of births and deaths in a state of balance; losses caused by deaths are more than replaced by births and population growth ensues. The actual degree to which growth takes place is seen as being largely related to the *carrying capacity* of the land, the state of the economy, and prevailing customs and attitudes. The argument proceeds that the prime aim in nearly all societies is to minimise the rate of mortality. As a consequence, the control of fertility is relegated to a secondary status. Where mortality is high, there is little need for the regulation of fertility. But when mortality is reduced to low levels, then the persistence of high fertility (and therefore of high rates of natural increase) will produce a scale of population growth which is eventually perceived as threatening to lower the general well-being of society. As a result, the regulation of fertility eventually becomes accepted as something needing to be undertaken for the collective good. The lowering of mortality rates, mainly through the conquest of disease and the

improvement of food supplies, seems to initiate the demographic transition; in time fertility rates are adjusted downwards in order to avoid runaway population growth.

At the start and finish of the demographic transition, the conditions are essentially stable; there is little natural change. Clearly, the key part of the transition is the time it takes for the fertility rate to respond to the fall in the mortality rate. In terms of population growth, the length of this *response time* is absolutely critical. Obviously, in a situation of high fertility and a rapidly falling mortality rate, there can be much population growth in a relatively short time. In the case of Britain, the response time was probably in the order of 130 years. In that time, between 1750 and 1880, population increased fourfold from 7.5 to 30 million (Fig. 3.2).

There will always be a response time, because the reduction in the fertility rate is always regarded as a reaction rather than a stimulus. Added to the time-lag is the fact that the response is not an automatic reflex. It involves social choice and change; society has to progress through a series of steps, all of which take time (Fig. 3.3). First, it takes time to realise, and to have confirmed, that the falling mortality rate is having an effect on

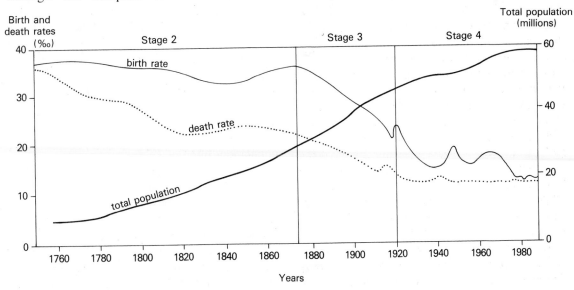

Figure 3.2 *The demographic transition in Great Britain (1750–1985)*

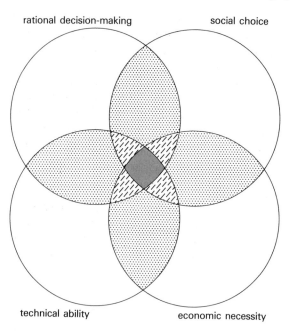

rational decision-making   social choice

technical ability   economic necessity

Figure 3.3 *Model of the preconditions for fertility decline*

population numbers. It then takes more time to become aware of the adverse consequences of those rising numbers. Presumably, if the economic necessity to reduce fertility is acute, this will hasten the process. Possible solutions to the problem need to be considered; an acceptable and technically feasible mode of fertility control has to be identified and then adopted. That process of adoption can be protracted, particularly if there is any form of resistance by groups opposed to the basic principle of birth control. Traditional attitudes and customs die hard, but eventually society is persuaded (if not forced) to change the basic norms or standards which it applies to population growth.

Foremost amongst such standards are those concerning what constitutes the ideal size of a *completed family*. In other words, how many surviving children should a couple ideally have when they reach the end of their reproductive period. If the concensus is that the ideal number is two, then there is the prospect of a stable population; above that number, there is the promise of population growth. If mortality

rates (particularly infant mortality) are high, then the couple must *overbear* in order to produce the ideal number of surviving children. Thus the argument proceeds that when the mortality rate falls, people have to make a double adjustment. They have to adjust to the reduction in the ideal family size required in order to lower the rate of population growth; they also have to reduce the established tendency to overbear. The fact that a double adjustment is necessary simply adds to the time required for the demographic transition; it adds to the length of that critical response time.

1 Better demographic data and more accurate forecasting of population growth.
2 Improved communications; more rapid diffusion of the need for regulation.
3 Modern society more dynamic and more amenable to social change.
4 Techniques for limiting fertility are now many, varied and cheap.
5 Major institutional groups now publicly favour fertility regulation.

Table 3.2 *Reasons for the reduction of the time-lag in the demographic transition*

Bogue (1969) has suggested that the response time today is likely to be much shorter than the British experience over a century ago. His reasons are summarised in Table 3.2. What seems certain is that modern society is more aware of, and better able to foresee, the demographic catastrophe that would occur if no attempt was made to control population growth (see Chapter 6). The theory of demographic regulation is simply a declaration of the belief that society will, when faced with serious overpopulation, often make the necessary adjustment to its fertility rather than leave nature to do the population pruning (hence the 'rational decision-making' shown in Figure 3.3). Certainly, it seems that fertility control by means of contraception is widely becoming an integral part of modern culture. Given that, and the impact of those factors listed in Table 3.2, it might be suggested that the speed and efficiency of the demographic transition process have been raised since Britain completed its transformation from high to low levels of fertility and mortality. Whether that suggestion is anything more than optimistic speculation is a question addressed later in this chapter and again in Chapter 6.

ASSIGNMENTS

4 Discuss why the reduction of the mortality rate should be regarded as a higher priority than the reduction of the fertility rate.

5 Exemplify each of the four pre-conditions for fertility decline shown in Figure 3.3.

6 Elaborate the reasons given in Table 3.2 for the possible shortening of the time taken for demographic transition.

THE DEMOGRAPHIC TRANSITION MODEL

Recognition of the process of demographic transition, and observations made of it in the more-developed countries of the world, particularly in Great Britain, have led population geographers to construct an idealised sequence of changes in the vital rates of a population. This sequence is known as the *demographic transition model*; it comprises four connected phases or stages (Fig. 3.4). Vital dimensions of

the model are shown in Figure 3.5. They are the crude birth, death and natural increase rates, infant mortality, life expectancy and age structure; also shown are three socio-economic indicators. The thinking behind the model is that all societies, although they may start at different times and progress at different rates, eventually experience the same sequence of demographic changes. Whilst there is a growing number of countries or societies which, following Britain and other West European nations, have now completed the transition, there remain a significant number which have scarcely made a start. The whole question of the universality of the model will be discussed later. For the moment, let us briefly describe the four phases of the model.

The high stationary stage

During this first stage, both the birth and death rates are high (Fig. 3.4). The latter tend to oscillate, reflecting the impact of recurrent famine, periodic wars and epidemics of infectious diseases. The losses of population, sustained during the times of increased mortality, are only just compensated by the gains when the mortality rate falls; therefore the population remains at a low, but fluctuating level. In Britain's case, this phase persisted until the middle of the eighteenth century. The evidence suggests that birth and death rates fluctuated between 30 and 40 per 1000.

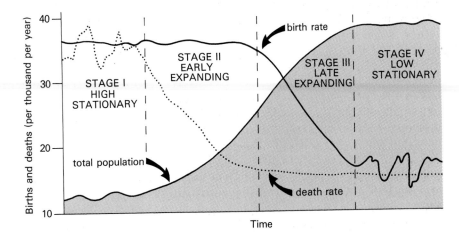

Figure 3.4 *The demographic transition model*

Figure 3.5 *Vital dimensions of the demographic transition, as illustrated by four sample countries*

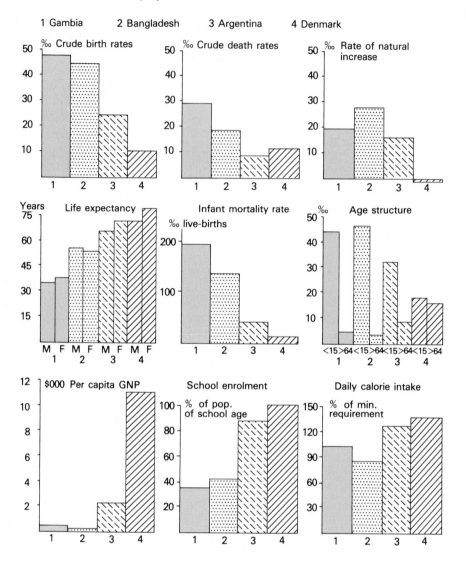

If we take a present-day example of a country deemed to be at Stage 1, we may deduce other vital aspects of the population. Gambia, in West Africa, remains as yet relatively untouched by development, except for a recent move into the tourist industry (Fig. 3.6). Its economy is still mainly concerned with subsistence agriculture and GNP per capita is as low as $230. It currently experiences a crude birth rate of just under 50 per 1000 and a crude death rate of just under 30, thus giving a natural increase rate of around 20 per 1000 (or 2 per cent per year). Possibly the worst aspects of the

demographic situation are the appallingly high infant mortality rate (193 deaths per 1000 live-births) and the low life expectancy (33.5 years for men, 36.5 for women). Reflecting the latter, as well as the high fertility, is the *age structure* of the population; 44 per cent of the population is aged under 15 years and only 4 per cent is aged over 65 (Fig. 3.5). But there are signs that the demographic situation is beginning to change. The total population, having remained fairly static up to 1970, has since started to expand. The key factor appears to have been a rise in the fertility rate rather than a fall in the mortality rate. According to the model, it would be the latter that would herald Gambia's progress to the next stage of the demographic transition.

The early expanding stage

The second stage is characterised by a continuing high birth rate, but a marked fall in the death rate (Fig. 3.4). The increasing divergence of these vital rates means high rates of natural increase and therefore considerable and accelerating population growth. Britain reached this stage in the late eighteenth century. The initial decline in the mortality rate was prompted by improved food supply and better diet, thanks to the advances embodied in the Agricultural Revolution (Fig. 3.2, p. 55). Another early contributory factor was the increased political stability of the country which brought with it a decline in the number of deaths resulting from civil wars and riots. Later, from the mid-nineteenth century onwards, reduction in the mortality rate was due rather more to improved housing and sanitation, better personal hygiene, and the application of advances in medical science. One immediate outcome of these developments was a marked decline in certain infectious diseases; by 1875 the death rate, having been more than halved, stood at about 15 per 1000. Why the birth rate remained so high for so long and why the rate did not fall with the decline in the rate of infant mortality are questions that are not easily answered. It may be that the economic conditions were encouraging, in the sense that expansion of the industrial economy was creating a huge demand for labour. Also making an impact was the social change of people marrying earlier than had previously been the case; this inevitably raised fertility levels. What we can be more certain about is the scale of the population growth that resulted from the increasing disparity between birth and death rates; between 1750 and 1875 population quadrupled, the highest annual rates of growth (> 1.77 per cent) being recorded during the 1820s.

Bangladesh serves as our contemporary case-

Figure 3.6 *Traditional handicrafts for sale in Gambia The rise of tourism is beginning to provide a basis for economic development in Gambia. The growing number of visitors, mainly escaping from the rigours of the European winter, are bringing in much needed foreign currency. The construction and running of the tourist infrastructure (hotels, restaurants, etc.) provides employment, whilst local artisans are waking up to the fact that there is money to be made in the souvenir trade.*

study of a country at Stage 2. At present, its crude birth and death rates stand at 45 and 17.5 per 1000 respectively, giving a natural increase rate of 27.5 per 1000 which is markedly higher than that for Gambia (Fig. 3.5). Total population, which now amounts to 101 million, has increased by over 50 per cent since 1965. Clearly contributing to that increase has been the lowering of the infant mortality rate (nonetheless, it still stands at 133 per 1000 live-births). Reflecting the overall decline in mortality are the life expectancy figures which are notably higher than those in Gambia. It is interesting to note that life expectancy for men is slightly higher than that for women. As such, this illustrates the point made on p. 46 (see also Table 2.6, p. 41) that the traditional demands made on women to bear large numbers of children tend to raise female mortality rates during the reproductive years. In terms of age structure, the population is very definitely a youthful one, with 46 per cent aged under 15 years and only 3 per cent aged over 64.

In Bangladesh the rise in population has created immense economic and social problems. The economy remains largely agricultural, producing a few primary products (such as jute, tea and tobacco) for the world market, and relying heavily on imports of manufactured goods. The GNP per capita figure of $170 is significantly lower than that for Gambia and clearly indicates the inability of the economy to provide a decent standard of living for the bulk of the population; the other two indicators confirm this impression (Fig. 3.5, p. 58). Thus Bangladesh finds itself in the *poverty trap* created when the mortality rate is lowered (thanks largely to imported medical aid), and the pace of economic development is outstripped by the consequent rate of population growth (Fig. 3.7). The case also emphasises the point made on p. 55, namely that this is the most crucial part of the demographic transition. The longer it takes the fertility rate to respond to the stimulus of a reduced mortality rate, the greater the population growth and the more overwhelming the sorts of problems that presently assail Bangladesh.

The late expanding stage

The beginning of Stage 3 is heralded by the first sustained fall in the birth rate; as fertility

Figure 3.7 *Homelessness and poverty in Bangladesh The two children belong to a family which has been forced to make its home in a railway truck. Homelessness is only one of a whole range of acute problems encountered in the towns and cities of Bangladesh; poverty, unemployment and a lack of social services are others. The urban populations, swollen by massive rural-urban migration and high rates of natural increase, are simply too large to be adequately supported.*

plunges, the decline in mortality begins to level off. The resulting progressive convergence of birth and death rates leads to a decline in the rate of natural increase and therefore a deceleration of population growth (Fig. 3.4, p. 57). In Britain's case, a falling birth rate characterised the period from 1875 to 1920, during which it was almost halved (Fig. 3.2, p. 55). The fall, although a key part of the demographic transition process, is not easily explained. In Britain and other European countries it seems to have been associated with the emergence of an increasingly urban society. In this society, the desire for (and perceived economic value of) large numbers of children in a family declined. Increasingly, children were (and still are) seen as a drain on financial resources and as a possible impediment to socio-economic advancement. Reinforcing that change in values was the availability of better methods of birth control. The levelling off of the death rate also needs explanation. The marked fall in the mortality rate during the preceding stage had been achieved by dealing with the more easily controlled causes of death. Notably, these were the *exogenetic causes* associated with environmental conditions. But once personal hygiene, sanitation and diet had been improved, further lowering of the mortality rate required the much tougher and slower task of tackling the more resistant and largely *endogenetic causes* of death. Nonetheless, by 1920 the British crude death rate was less than 15 per 1000.

Argentina today is probably about half-way through Stage 3. The crude birth rate is now 24 per 1000 and the death rate 8.5 per 1000, giving a natural increase rate of 15.5 per 1000 (Fig. 3.5, p. 58). It is interesting that the death rate is lower than that experienced in Britain when it reached the end of this stage. The difference is probably explained by the progress made since in medicine which has certainly depressed the rate of infant mortality. But whatever the explanation, clearly the impact is significant; Argentina currently experiences double the rate of population growth (2.0 per cent per annum) that Britain did some 80 years ago when it was at the equivalent stage in the demographic transition. Life expectancy is markedly higher than in Bangladesh, being 65 years for men and 72 years for women. This is reflected in the age structure, with 31 per cent aged under 15 and 8 per cent aged over 64. The three socio-economic indicators suggest a rather better situation than in Bangladesh, despite the fact that the Argentinian economy lacks a substantial manufacturing base; 70 per cent of its export earnings are accounted for by agricultural products (Fig. 3.8). In this respect, the case of

Figure 3.8 *Loading beef exports at Buenos Aires*
The economy of Argentina is heavily dependent on the export of pastoral and arable products; industrialisation has been largely confined to food-processing and textiles. In recent years, the appearance of food surpluses on the world market has lowered commodity prices, which in turn have debilitated the Argentinian economy. This downturn, in combination with a high rate of natural increase, now threatens to lower living standards.

Argentina differs from that of Britain, which by 1920 was already a highly industrialised and urbanised country.

The low stationary stage

The beginning of this stage is marked by the levelling out of the birth rate curve and the stage as a whole is characterised by low birth and death rates (Fig. 3.4, p. 57). Consequently, there are low rates of natural increase and little population growth. The flattening of Britain's population curve has been most marked during the last intercensal period, when the growth rate was a mere 0.05 per cent per annum (Fig. 3.2, p. 55). Also diagnostic of this stage is the stability of the death rate; during peace time it has remained at or around 12 per 1000. In contrast, the birth rate has been more prone to fluctuations, tending to rise and fall with the booms and recessions in the economy, as well as showing a 'bulge' after each of the two world wars. The fluctuations have been within the range of 12 to 18 per 1000. The fertility rate has been kept at a low level by prevailing social attitudes about the desirability of family limitation. Thus there is widespread practice of birth control, made that much more effective by the efficiency of modern contraceptive methods and by the legalisation of abortion.

Although Britain may have been one of the first countries to complete the demographic transition and to reach Stage 4, there is evidence to suggest that it may now have been overtaken. Other countries are now showing even lower vital rates. In Denmark, for example, the crude birth rate is only 10 per 1000 and is exceeded by the crude death rate of just over 11 per 1000 (Fig. 3.5, p. 58). Thus Denmark has moved into a situation of natural decrease. It is not unique in this respect (West Germany and Hungary are two other cases), whilst there are rather more countries where the rate of natural increase is a fraction of 1 per 1000 (examples are Austria, Belgium, Luxembourg and Sweden). Perhaps surprising is the fact that the crude death rate of Denmark is higher than in Argentina. This is simply

explained by the older or greyer population structure of Denmark, with 15 per cent of its population aged over 64 and only 18 per cent below the age of 15. Also noteworthy is the low level of infant mortality; in many European countries it is now less than 10 per 1000 live-births. Life expectancy has risen to 72 for men and 78 for women; but higher values are to be found elsewhere. In both Sweden and Japan, the values are 74 and 80. The three socio-economic indicators suggest that superior conditions prevail when a country reaches Stage 4; the essentially stationary population makes it relatively easy for economic development to sustain a good quality of life (Fig. 3.9). But Stage 4 is not without its problems. Affluence, by encouraging excessive consumption of food and drink, raises the morbidity rates, especially of heart and liver disease. The increased ageing of the population heightens the demand for the social services that benefit the elderly; it also places a greater burden on the economically active (see Chapter 5). At the same time, the birth rate fluctuations make it difficult to plan the proper provision of things like maternity beds in hospitals, school places and work opportunities.

ASSIGNMENTS

7 a. Explain the significance of the three socio-economic indicators (per capita GNP, school enrolment and daily calorie intake) used in Figure 3.5.

  b. Which appears to fit best with the stages of the demographic transition, and why might this be so?

8 With reference to Stage 1 of the demographic transition model, explain why the crude birth rate fluctuates more than the death rate.

9 Suggest ways in which governments might intervene to speed up the passage of Stage 2 of the demographic transition model.

10 With reference to Stage 3 of the demographic transition model, explain:

  a. the rapid decline in the birth rate.

  b. the slow decline in the death rate.

11 Why did the birth rates of many countries rise immediately after the two world wars?

Figure 3.9 *Affluent shoppers in Copenhagen*
Zero population growth and a stable, balanced economy are key factors in Denmark's high ranking as one of the world's most prosperous nations. But for all the high living standards, the material comfort and the personal affluence, there are clear indications that these achievements have not made the Danish people immune to the stresses of modern living. The relatively high incidence of depression and suicide are two such indicators.

12 From a source, such as the *United Nations Demographic Yearbook*, collect the vital statistics for two or more countries. Plot them as in Figure 3.3 and assess the current position of those countries along the demographic transition model.

THE MODEL REVIEWED

It should be stressed at the outset that the demographic transition model is no more than a broad generalisation. It simply depicts a pattern and path of change which, it is argued, will be followed by nearly all countries (Fig. 3.4, p. 57). Figure 3.10 shows the progress of the demographic transition in Europe during the nineteenth and early-twentieth centuries. It serves to illustrate three important features. First, that the regions within a country will not necessarily all reach the same stage together. For example, regional differences in the attainment of Stage 3 are to be seen within Britain, Italy and Spain. This is partly explained by the fact that not all the regions of those countries started the transition at the same time. The same observation also holds true at a national level. Clearly, France was well ahead of the rest

Figure 3.10 *The progress of the demographic transition in Europe (1840–1920)*

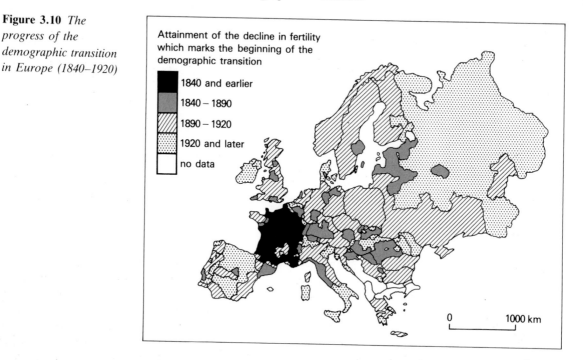

of Europe in reaching Stage 3. This leads to the second feature: at any point in time, countries and their regions may be compared in terms of the progress they have made along the demographic transition. Putting these two features together enables us to identify a third, namely that countries and regions may also be compared according to their speed in completing the demographic transition. As regards this speed, it has already become evident in other parts of the world that those countries now in the early stages of the model are progressing at a faster rate than was the case with most of the European countries that have now completed the transition. This is hardly surprising, bearing in mind that those behind benefit from the experience of those who have gone before. The greatly improved availability of modern science and technology, even in the less-developed countries, has helped to speed things up; as has the aid extended to Third World countries. However, this observed quickening of pace in no way invalidates the generalisation embodied in the model; nor does it alter the pattern of change; it simply reduces the time scale.

The model clearly has a practical value in

that it provides a sound basis for forecasting, in broad terms, what changes are likely to occur in the demographic situation of a country over a specified period. For those countries in the transition from Stage 1 to Stage 2, the model provides a clear warning to governments. This is that they should devise prompt and effective measures to lower fertility rates as quickly as possible, so shortening the length of Stage 2 with its promise of high rates of population growth. It should also be noted that the rate of population growth threatens to be much faster today than was the experience of Britain in the nineteenth century. Given the availability of modern methods of death control, the mortality rate will be likely to fall more abruptly and to even lower levels, thereby giving a sort of double boost to population growth. It is during this stage that there is the greatest risk of *overpopulation* (see Chapter 6).

It is tempting to relate the stages of the demographic transition to *modernisation*, particularly to the state of economic development. Indeed, some possible relationships were indicated during the previous section. In a sense there is no harm in doing so, provided it is

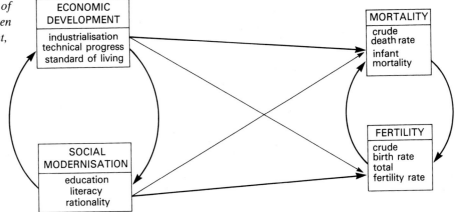

Figure 3.11 *A model of the associations between economic development, social modernisation, mortality and fertility*

clearly understood that the relationship is not necessarily a causal one. The demographic transition is certainly not the stimulus of economic development. That economic development might be the cause of the demographic transition in the British case seems a plausible one. But the initial lowering of mortality in many parts of the tropical world during the second half of this century, as in Bangladesh, points to a rather different stimulus. The case-studies of Argentina and Denmark make another important point, namely that progress through the transition does not require the high levels of industrialisation and urbanisation that appear to have propelled Britain beyond Stage 2. In France, Japan and Sweden, for example, the reduction of fertility rates which mark Stage 3 had no connection with industrialisation. In France, the stimulus was the Revolution (1789) which promoted the idea of what is called *social capillarity* – the belief that one's children can rise in social status if their number is reduced. In Japan and Sweden, the move to smaller families was stimulated by the inheritance laws which required that landholdings had to be equally divided between the offspring of a deceased person. Curbing family size was one obvious way of reducing the uneconomic fragmentation of land.

It is case studies such as these that lead modern population geographers to make the distinction between *economic development* and *social modernisation* when analysing the poss-

ible association between the broad development of a country and its progress along the demographic transition. Whilst they are prepared to concede that economic growth has, in many instances, been a prime mover in lowering mortality rates, they prefer to link the lowering of fertility rates rather more to social modernisation. The model in Figure 3.11 illustrates these potent associations. It also shows strong positive links between economic development and social modernisation, and between mortality and fertility. In contrast, the links between economic development and fertility, and between social modernisation and mortality are shown to be weaker. But this is not to exclude the possibility that the recent reductions in mortality rates referred to earlier are not the outcome, in part at least, of social modernisation.

Whilst the existence of a causal link between the demographic transition and development needs to be qualified, there is wide acceptance that part of the association is especially significant. This is the relationship between the rate of economic development and the rate of population growth at any given point in the transition. It is a crucial influence on the general well-being of a population. When the two rates rise in harmony, there is little to worry about; but when population growth strides ahead of economic development, then there is the prospect of lower standards of living. This is the critical relationship to be explored in Chapter 6.

One final point to be made is this. At the moment, the demographic histories of the most advanced countries allow us to define four broad stages. What of the future? Can we assume that Stage 4, once reached, lasts for ever? Looking at recent demographic trends in those countries, there may be grounds for suggesting the onset of a fifth stage in the model – a low contracting stage – characterised by low mortality, fertility below the replacement rate, and therefore natural decrease and declining population. Should that stage materialise, however, it will not invalidate the model; the model would simply be extended.

ASSIGNMENTS

---

13 Explain why, in the case of Britain, there may have been a causal link between economic development and the beginning of the demographic transition.

14 Explain what might have initiated the lowering of mortality rates in those countries which have only recently started to make the demographic transition.

15 With reference to Figure 3.11, explore the links between:

 a. economic development and social modernisation

 b. social modernisation and fertility.

AN OVERVIEW OF THE GLOBAL DEMOGRAPHIC SITUATION

The aim of this section is to demonstrate one particularly geographical value of the demographic transition model. Using the four stages contained in the model, it is possible to devise a simple classification scheme which can be applied to all the countries of the world. In essence, each stage is marked by a particular set of demographic characteristics which combine to give rise to a distinctive type and scale of population growth. For example, Stage 1 countries are distinguished by slow population growth; Stage 2 by accelerating growth; Stage 3 by high, but decelerating, growth; and Stage 4 by very low rates of growth and, in some instances, even by population decline. The demographic transition model shows that the main determinant of the type of population growth is the nature of the balance between the rates of fertility and mortality. Thus when we come to apply the fourfold classification, it is easier if we define each category by fairly precise values for the crude birth and death rates. This has been done in preparing Figure 3.12. High fertility is assumed to exist at a crude birth rate greater than 35 per 1000; moderate fertility between 20 and 35; and low fertility below 20. For mortality, the equivalent threshold values are 22 and 12 per 1000. What has to be admitted is the degree of subjectivity involved in arriving at these critical values. Clearly, there is scope for questioning whether particular thresholds might be slightly higher or lower; but in general terms, these values would appear to be broadly right for the global demographic situation in the mid-1980s. It is interesting to point out that Broek and Webb (1968) used birth rate values of 35 and 25, and death rate values of 25 and 15 when analysing the situation in the mid-1960s.

Looking at Figure 3.12, it is clear that there are relatively few countries which are still at Stage 1 and have yet to embark on the demographic transition. Apart from Afghanistan and Yemen, all are located in Africa; all are classified by the World Bank as 'low-income economies'. The demographic transition model depicts these Stage 1 countries as having stationary populations. However, mid-year estimates of population made over the last two decades clearly indicate an upward trend in numbers. Over the period 1973 to 1985, the population growth rate averaged around 2 per cent per annum. This growth may be explained by the fact that, although rates of fertility and mortality are both high by global standards, there is nonetheless a difference between them. In some countries, such as Angola, Niger and Sierra Leone, the natural increase rate is as

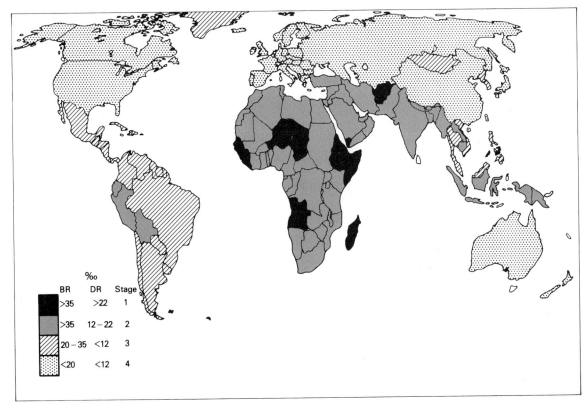

Figure 3.12 *The demographic situation, by country (1985)*

high as 25 per 1000. Although fluctuating on an almost annual basis, there appears to have been an upward drift in fertility, and a downward drift in mortality. These countries still await the plummet in the rate of mortality that marks the beginning of Stage 2; most also await economic development (Fig. 3.13). Reflecting the latter is the prevalence of low GNP per capita; in most cases, it is substantially less than $400 (Fig. 3.14).

It is Africa which dominates the distribution

Figure 3.13 *Primitive farming in Burkina Faso Economic development in Burkina Faso is still little more than subsistence agriculture. With the rate of natural increase currently around 26 per 1000, there is every prospect that food production will be unable to satisfy increased needs and that per capita GNP will fall to below $150, making Burkina Faso one of the poorest countries in the world.*

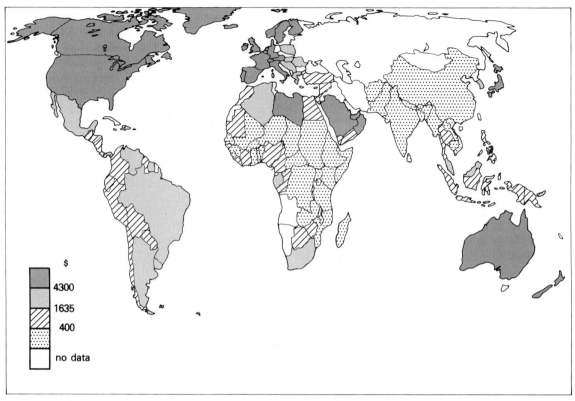

Figure 3.14 *Gross national product per capita, by country (1985)*

of those countries at Stage 2 of the model (Fig. 3.12), although the Middle East, South and South East Asia and a belt in South America also feature. With fertility maintained at a high level and the rate of mortality declining, these are the countries experiencing the fastest rates of population growth. In quite a number of cases, the natural increase rates exceed 30 per 1000 and for the period 1973–1985 the mean annual population growth rate was in excess of 3 per cent. For example, the figures are 37 and 4.3 respectively for Botswana, and 34 and 3.6 for Iraq. Clearly, it is these Stage 2 countries which are most vulnerable to *overpopulation* (Fig. 3.15). Nowhere is there greater need for government programmes to reduce fertility and to boost economic development. As regards the latter, nearly all the countries are in the World Bank categories of 'low- and middle-income economies'; GNP per capita values show quite a wide range, from less than $400 to over $4000

in 'high-income oil exporters' like Libya and Saudi Arabia (Fig. 3.14). Possibly the most worrying aspect is the fact that this category includes some of the most populous countries in the world today. Examples include India (765 million), Indonesia (162 million). Bangladesh (101 million) and Nigeria (100 million). Altogether, Stage 2 countries account for over 40 per cent of the world's population. In short, with a mean annual growth rate of 3 per cent, huge additions are being made each year to the size of the global population.

Latin America dominates the distribution of countries currently passing through Stage 3. Apart from Albania and Greenland, the remaining countries in this category (Mongolia, Thailand, Malaysia, Philippines and the two Koreas) are all located in Asia. What needs to be stressed is that in some of these countries, although there has been a downward trend in

Figure 3.15 *Environmental degradation in Burkina Faso*
Overpopulation almost inevitably generates environmental costs. In this case, trees have been overbrowsed by grazing livestock and then either ruthlessly mutilated to provide fuel and building materials or cleared to increase the cultivated area. Deforestation, in its turn, disrupts the hydrological cycle and ultimately leads to desertification.

fertility, current crude birth rates remain quite high (often over 25 per 1000). This, in conjunction with a continuing reduction of the mortality rate brought about by modernisation, has meant the persistence of moderate to high rates of natural increase (frequently in excess of 20 per 1000). Recent annual rates of population growth average around 2.5 per cent.

Examples are Brazil (2.3 per cent), Mexico (2.8 per cent) and Thailand (2.2 per cent). The prospects for a further lowering of the fertility rate are somewhat limited, given that Roman Catholicism is the dominant religion in most of these countries (Fig. 3.16). But on the brighter side, these countries account for less than 10 per cent of the world's population and the

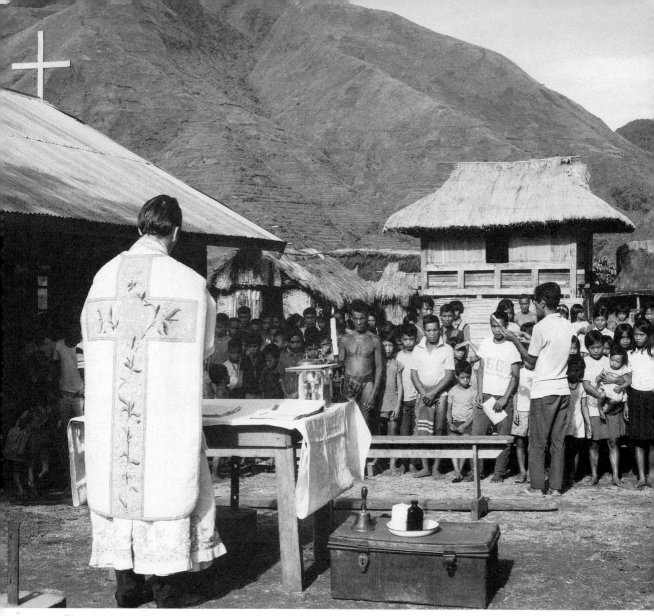

Figure 3.16 *A Roman Catholic mass being held in a Philippines village*
The Roman Catholic Church holds very strong views on the subject of birth control, being firmly opposed to contraception and willing only to countenance family planning when effected by means of abstinence. Given that Roman Catholicism probably has more adherents in the world than any other religion, the demographic repercussions of its teachings, particularly in more primitive societies, must be considerable.

majority have made considerable strides in terms of economic development; per capita GNP values tend to be above $1500 (Fig. 3.14). In this sense, then, they are better able to cope with population growth than many of the Stage 2 countries.

Countries at Stage 4 account for approximately 50 per cent of the global land area and 48 per cent of the world population (Fig. 3.12, p.67). This is perhaps the most comforting aspect of the present global demographic situation, for it can be said that literally half the world has its population under reasonable control. Crude birth rates are often below 15 per 1000 and crude death rates not much less; rates of natural increase are low (usually below 10 per

Figure 3.17 *24-hour cash dispensers in Hong Kong*
These money machines epitomise the prosperity of the world's leading economies. Not only is there a seemingly endless availability of cash and credit, but successful advertising and product promotion have convinced people that they need to part with their money in order to acquire, day or night, a whole range of non-essential goods and services.

1000); and little population growth (less than 1 per cent per annum) prevails. Adding to the general well-being of these countries is their advanced economic development. Most of the World Bank's 'industrial market' and 'East European non-market' economies have reached Stage 4 (Fig. 3.17). One notable exception is China, qualifying for Stage 4 mainly by virtue of its stringent population policies which have halved the birth rate to 18.5 per 1000 over the last 20 years (Fig. 2.8, p. 37). With GNP per capita at only $310, as compared with $11 330 for neighbouring Japan, clearly China has a long way to go before its people can enjoy the same material conditions as the people in Europe, North America and Australasia (Fig. 3.14).

ASSIGNMENTS

16 Give reasons why you might expect the critical values used in the compilation of Figure 3.12 to be different from those used 20 years before.

17 Make a detailed comparison of Figures 3.12 and 3.14. To what extent does there appear to be a relationship between the two sets of variables?

18 Combining the information given in Figures 3.12 and 3.14, try to design a classification that might be applied to all the countries of the world.

19 a. With reference to Figure 3.15, explain in detail how deforestation leads to desertification.

   b. Discover other ways in which overpopulation can cause environmental damage.

CONCLUSION

It might be claimed that the demographic transition is one of the most profound changes to affect any country. Particularly critical are its speed, the scale of population growth which it generates, and whether or not this growth is matched by economic and social advancement (a key relationship to be explored in Chapter 6). The fact that the demographic transition is something which happens to virtually all countries allows us to devise a demographic transition model, along which we can chart the progress of countries as they move from high to low levels of fertility and mortality. The model also provides a basis for comparing and classifying countries. From this it becomes possible, as in Figure 3.12 (p. 67), to analyse the global demographic situation in terms of the present distribution of different scales of population growth. Perhaps even more important, it provides a basis for forecasting the likely pattern of future growth that will emerge as individual countries make further progress along the demographic transition.

ASSIGNMENTS

20 Explain how the demographic transition model might be used to forecast:
a. the amount of world population growth between now and the year 2000
b. the global distribution of that growth.

4

Population on the Move

DEFINITIONS AND CLASSIFICATION

The population change equation

Two basic points have been stressed in the last two chapters. First, that the number of people living in a given area fluctuates over time; and secondly, that this rise and fall in numbers can be explained by changes in the rate of natural increase. There is, of course, another possible contributor to the change in total population – the movement of people from one area to another. We need to reiterate the point made in Chapter 2 (Fig. 2.2, p. 30) that this movement can reinforce the trend in population resulting from a change in the rate of natural increase (i.e. an alteration of the balance between birth and death rates). For example, where an area is already experiencing population growth from natural increase, an influx of people from another area will clearly push the rate of growth even higher. Equally, an outward movement of people will accelerate the decline in numbers caused by deaths exceeding births. Population movements can also act as a counterbalance. For instance, a low rate of natural increase, or even a naturally declining population, might be supplemented by an inward movement of people; whilst the increasing numbers created by a high rate of natural increase might be reduced by an outward movement. In this way, population movements become an important component of population change, as is shown by the *population change equation*:

$$PC = NI + NM$$

$$\text{or } (B - D) + NM$$

where *PC* (population change) over a given period is a function of *NI* (natural increase) or *B − D* (births minus deaths) and *NM* (net migration).

The classification of mobility

Population movements range in scale and distance from a shopping visit, or the moving of a single person from one flat to another within the same town, to the mass movements of people across international frontiers and between continents. They can also differ with respect to time. Some movements are continuous and regular, such as the daily commuting of workers or the seasonal shifts of tribes whose livelihood depends on migrating animals. Other movements are more one-off and permanent, as when Jewish people have moved to Israel. Between these extremes there are semi-permanent movements, as undertaken by shifting cultivators in Amazonia or by workers on fixed-term contracts overseas (Fig. 4.1, overleaf).

It is common practice to refer to all population movements under the general heading of migration. However, the United Nations Organisation (UNO) has recommended that in national censuses the term *migration* should be used only to describe those movements which involve people moving from one administrative area to another, and which result in a permanent change of residence. Thus the distinction is drawn between *migration* and *circulation* (Fig. 4.2). The former results in *displacement*. The latter involves *reciprocal flows* and includes typically short-term, repetitive or cyclical movements without a permanent or long-standing change of residence. Shopping, commuting, pastoral nomadism and shifting

Figure 4.1 *Four different forms of mobility*
Moving home **(a)** *is the essence of migration, but in the case of nomadism* **(b)**, *the mobility is so continuous that it is classified as circulation. Purchasing food, be it in the market place* **(c)** *or from a shop, is possibly the most widespread and common form of circulation, followed by commuting, be it to a regular job in a city-centre or casual work on a farm* **(d)**.

a

b

c

d

Figure 4.2 *The distinction between migration and circulation*

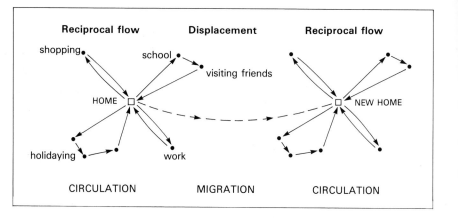

cultivation would, for example, be regarded as instances of *circulation*. In population geography, *mobility* is the umbrella term used to embrace all population movements, that is both migration and circulation.

The distinction between migration and circulation is fundamental and frequently provides the basic subdivision in classifications of population mobility. However, the definition of migration poses two difficulties. The first concerns the UNO reference to administrative areas and the need for migration to involve movement across an administrative boundary. What is the smallest administrative unit in order for a movement to qualify as migration? If it is a local government area, then the term migration will not include those large numbers of permanent changes of residence that take place as households move from one part of a town to another. The second difficulty concerns the definition of *permanent residence*. For international standardisation, the UNO has stipulated a duration of at least one year before residence qualifies as being 'permanent'. In the opinion of many, this is thought to be too short a time. It certainly leads to some confusion when circulation involves periods of absence from home exceeding a year. For example, the Black workers drawn to South Africa from neighbouring states by the job opportunities in mines and factories can stay there for several years. But it is neither their intention, nor that of the South African Government, that they should become permanent residents. Those

workers are simply part of a regular circulation to and from South Africa.

Duration of residence is only one of a number of criteria that may be used in classifying population movements. Unfortunately, there is as yet no universal classification, but Figure 4.3 suggests one possible scheme. Migration and circulation are the first-order division. Circulation is quite readily subdivided according to the frequency of the circulation: daily, periodic, seasonal and long-term. It would be equally valid to classify types of circulation on the basis of purpose – subsistence, employment, education, shopping, entertainment, etc. The classification of migration is more complicated. There are many possible criteria, such as distance, direction, volume, cause and the nature of the decision-making process. Such measures interrelate and overlap, and call for subjective judgement in saying which of them is the more important. In Figure 4.3, the distinction between forced and voluntary migrations is thought to be fundamental; that between national and international then acknowledges the importance of state boundaries. The third tier in the classification emphasises the directional distinction: urban and rural nationally, and developed world and developing world internationally.

The classification shown in Figure 4.3 is no more than one person's view of how population mobility might be analysed. Alternative schemes might be equally, if not more, valid and useful. The scheme here may certainly be criticised, if

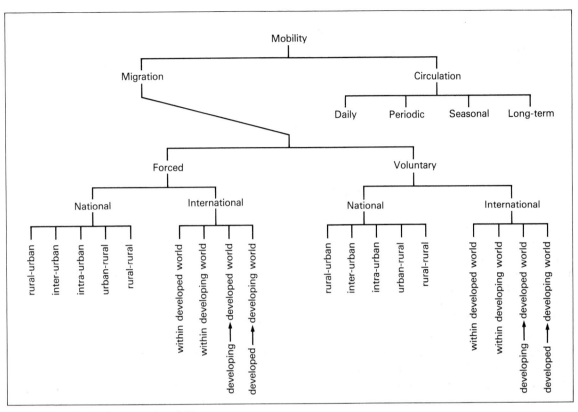

Figure 4.3 *A classification of mobility*

only on the grounds that it has omitted to use some important migration characteristics, such as volume, motives and duration. But at least this scheme fulfils the basic aim of all classification; it imposes some sort of order and structure on a mass of differences, in this instance, on the huge variety of population movements.

Some basic terminology

There are some terms used in the study of mobility that might usefully be defined at this point. People involved in the same migration form a *migration stream*. Where there is a two-way movement between areas, the stronger migration stream is called the *dominant migration* and the weaker movement in the opposite direction the *reverse* or *counter-migration*. In the study of such two-way migration, the total volume of movement is known as the *gross*

interchange, whilst the difference between the opposing movements is the *net interchange*.

Migrants who cross international boundaries are referred to as *emigrants* in the country of origin and *immigrants* in the country of destination. Where the migration takes place within a country, but across administrative boundaries, the equivalent terms are *out-migrant* and *in-migrant*. For any area, the difference between the number of arrivals (immigrants and/or in-migrants) and the number of departing people (out-migrants and/or emigrants) is known as either *net migration* or the *net migration balance*. If arrivals exceed departures, then the balance is *positive*; if the reverse situation applies, the balance is *negative*. *Gross migration* is the total volume of movement both into and out of an area (i.e. all immigrants, emigrants, in-migrants and out-migrants). The relationship between gross migration and net migration is, along with the ratio between dominant and reverse migration, taken as a measure of the *efficiency of migration*. Basically, the smaller the relative difference between gross and net migration in a given area, and the greater the difference between dominant and reverse migrations, the greater the efficiency of migration i.e. the greater the net redistribution of people.

ASSIGNMENTS

1 Discuss how you might improve the official definition of migration.
2 Devise your own classification of population movements, possibly using different criteria. Compare its merits with those of the scheme shown in Figure 4.3.
3 Give an actual example of each of the following categories of migration shown in Figure 4.3:
   a. the four subtypes of forced, international migration
   b. the five subtypes of voluntary, internal migration.
4 Suggest circumstances in which it would be helpful to have a measure of the efficiency of migration.

THE MAINSPRING OF MIGRATION

People migrate for a wide range of reasons and most people will migrate at least once during their lifetime. For instance, migration might first take place when parents move to a larger house to accommodate better their growing family. Later on, migration might occur when the young adult decides to go to some distant university or polytechnic. Starting work is another time in the *life-cycle* when migration is likely to take place, as also is marriage. Then a whole succession of moves might follow associated with promotion at work, with having children that increase the need for household space, and with increasing affluence. Retirement is also commonly marked by migration as

people move to be near their children or settle into a smaller house in a pleasant environment. Even later on, there is the possibility of a move into some form of sheltered housing.

The push-pull model

Whatever the reasons and no matter the timing in the life-cycle, most migration is the outcome of two sets of forces. *Push* forces work in the migrant's home area. These are pressures which persuade the person to move away and might include the impact of natural disasters (drought, floods, famine), low wages, persecution and civil war. The *pull* forces are those which attract the migrant to a particular destination. Good social and welfare services, a pleasant environment and political freedom are typical pull factors (Fig. 4.4a).

Broadly speaking, push and pull factors fall into four categories: physical, economic, social, and political (Table 4.1). Quite often, a sort of complementarity will exist between particular push and pull factors. For example, unemployment and poor housing in the area of departure might match up with the availability of job opportunities and cheap, modern housing in the area of arrival. Such complementarity might be seen as strengthening the likelihood of migration taking place between the areas concerned.

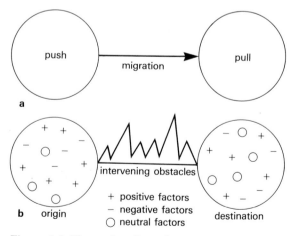

Figure 4.4 *The push-pull mechanism:*
(a) *the simple model*
(b) *Lee's model*

In other cases, however, this complementarity will not exist to any great degree. Instead, migration will be motivated by either a dominant push factor, such as a natural disaster or a civil war, in so-called *forced migrations*; or an overwhelmingly strong pull factor, such as the offer of a new job overseas at a greatly increased salary.

	Push	Pull
Physical	inaccessibility	
	harsh climate	
	natural disaster	
		scenic quality
		fertile soils
		lack of natural hazards
Economic	unemployment	
	poverty	
	high rents	
	heavy taxes	
		high living standards
		good wages
		promotion
		resource exploitation
Social	discrimination	
	lack of housing	
	bereavement	
	growth of family	
		good welfare services
		relatives and friends
		marriage
		higher education
Political	civil unrest	
	persecution	
	planning decision	
		freedom of speech
		propaganda
		political asylum

Table 4.1 *Some reasons for migration*

Migration and the individual

Studies of migration tend to emphasise its general aspects – its patterns, streams and reasons. In doing so, it is easy to overlook, particularly in so-called *voluntary migration*, that the decision to migrate rests with the individual. Whether or not to move, where to move, when to move, and how to move are all questions mainly resolved by personal decision-making. For this reason, we might regard the migration stream as the aggregate outcome of the decisions made by a large number of individuals. Each decision will be based on the perception of the complex interaction of push and pull factors. But people react differently to the same push and pull factors, since they perceive and evaluate the same pressures and attractions differently. Some people are highly responsive to these forces and will readily migrate, whilst others need a much stronger stimulus before deciding to move. Figure 4.5 gives some indication of the decision-making process involved in moving house. This acknowledgement of individuality and of personal perception in the context of migration decision-making is referred to as *migration elasticity*.

The information which a person has about potential destinations is also crucial to understanding and explaining migration behaviour. The quantity and quality of that information, referred to as the *information field*, will vary enormously from person to person. The information will be both limited and biased; rarely, if ever, does the decision-making involve an objective assessment of attributes. The information field displays a *distance-decay* characteristic, in that the knowledge of areas lessens with increasing distance from the present place of residence. Information about distant places will include what is learnt through visits and the mass-media, but more influential perhaps will be communication with friends and relatives who happen to live in distant places. If these people happen also to have been migrants themselves, then the information which they pass back could well persuade the would-be migrant to follow suit, so establishing a *migration chain*. After the Second World War, migration chains were clearly evident in the Indian emigration to the United Kingdom. In this instance, the links were forged, not only by the feedback of information and by kinship ties, but also by money being sent back to the Indian subcontinent to

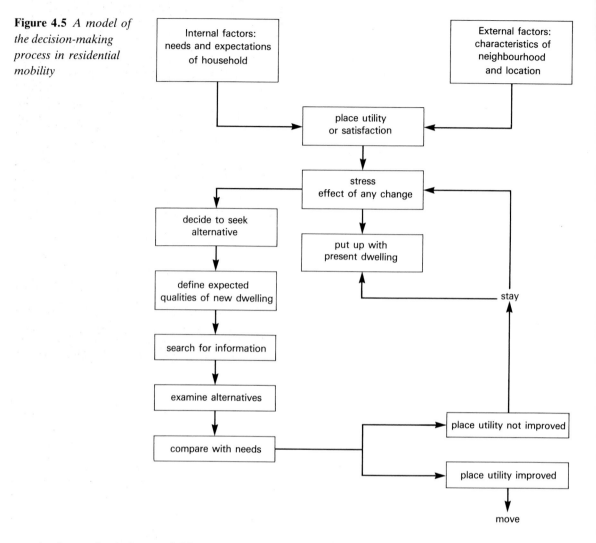

Figure 4.5 *A model of the decision-making process in residential mobility*

pay the fares of relatives and friends wishing to follow the same migration route (Fig. 4.6).

The information field acquired by an individual will enable that person to draw a *mental map*, a personal view of the world, which might include some evaluation of potential destinations. Figure 4.7 shows the mental preference images of British school-leavers in Bristol and in Inverness, who were asked to indicate where they would prefer to live. In both cases, the preference for the local area was consistent with the distance-decay characteristic of information fields. However, equally impressive were the exceptions, where rather more distant locations were preferred. Presumably the

renown of areas like the Lake District and the south coast was so great as to counteract the friction of distance.

The Lee model

It was because of migration elasticity that Lee (1966) revised the simple push-pull model (Fig. 4.4b, p. 78). He does not attempt to isolate particular push and pull factors as influencing personal migrational decisions; rather, he sees both the place of origin and the place of destination as possessing a range of attributes. Each individual perceives these attributes differently, depending on personal characteristics like age,

complem...
facto...
(e.g. la...

governi...
polici...
(e.g. ta...

social sy...
(e.g. de...
unit)

urban ...

self-emp...
earni...

probab...
of a...

Figure 4.6 *Indian immigrants arriving at Victoria Station, London in 1959*
These people were part of the first-wave of New Commonwealth immigrants to enter the United Kingdom after the Second World War. Coming mainly from India, Pakistan and the Caribbean islands, they were drawn principally by the employment opportunities created by post-war reconstruction and the rising tide of economic prosperity. Once established, not just in London but in other cities as far apart as Bristol and Bradford, these immigrants soon stimulated the establishment of clearly-defined migration chains.

Figure 4...

migratio...
4.8 is o...
the con...

5 Refer...
   a. Ide...
      the...
   b. Su...
      no...
6 With...
   a. W...
      Ju...
   b. Su...
      im...
7 Expla...
   what...
   in Fig...

Figure 4.7 *Mental preference images in Britain:*
(a) *school leavers in Bristol*
(b) *school leavers in Inverness*

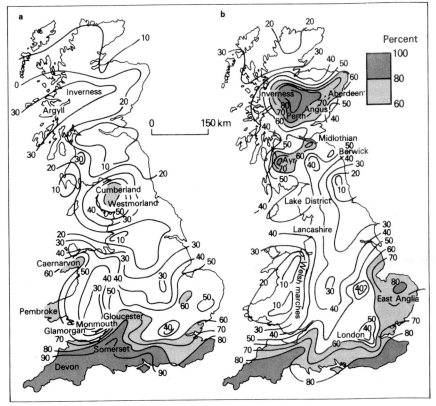

Migration volume

Perhaps the best known of Ravenstein's laws stated that 'most migrants travel short distances and that with increasing distance the numbers of migrants decrease'. In short, migration is a *distance-decay* phenomenon. Ravenstein's reasoning was that areas immediately adjacent to an area of in-migration are likely to provide more migrants than areas further away, since migration from more distant places would be precluded by the greater cost of travel and by less awareness of the opportunities. Zipf (1946) later put this notion in a rather more sophisticated way. His *inverse distance law* stated that 'the volume of migration is inversely proportional to the distance travelled by the migrants,' as expressed by the formula:

$$Mij = \frac{1}{dij}$$

where *Mij* is the number of migrants moving between places *i* and *j* and *dij* is the distance between those two places. If the results derived by applying this formula are plotted on a graph with arithmetic scales, a reverse J-curve is produced (Fig. 4.9a). It clearly shows that, with increasing distance, the volume of migration decreases at a faster and faster rate. The relationship between the two variables is referred to as a *negative exponential* one; if it were plotted on a graph using logarithmic scales, it would appear as a straight line (Fig. 4.9b).

Zipf's law was later refined when it was realised that the volume of migration between two places was also dependent on the sizes of their respective populations. In other words, the larger the populations, the greater the volume of migration. The larger the population of the area of origin, the larger will be the potential supply of migrants; the larger the population of the area of destination, the greater will be the migrant reception potential. This revised view of migration is expressed by the basic *gravity model* formula:

$$Mij = \frac{pi,\, pj}{dij^2}$$

where *M* is the volume of migration between places *i* and *j*, *pi* the population of place *i*, *pj* the population of place *j* and *dij* is the distance between them, usually raised by an exponent of 2. This gravity model formula also takes into account another of Ravenstein's laws, noted on p. 77, namely that most migration streams produce a compensating counter-current of reverse migration.

This is reflected in a rather different view of migration put forward by Stouffer (1960). He suggested that the volume of migration between two places is related not so much to distance and population size, but to perceived opportunities which exist in those two places and between them. Stouffer's *theory of intervening opportunities* states that the amount of migration over a given distance is directly proportional to the number of opportunities at the place of destination, and inversely proportional to the

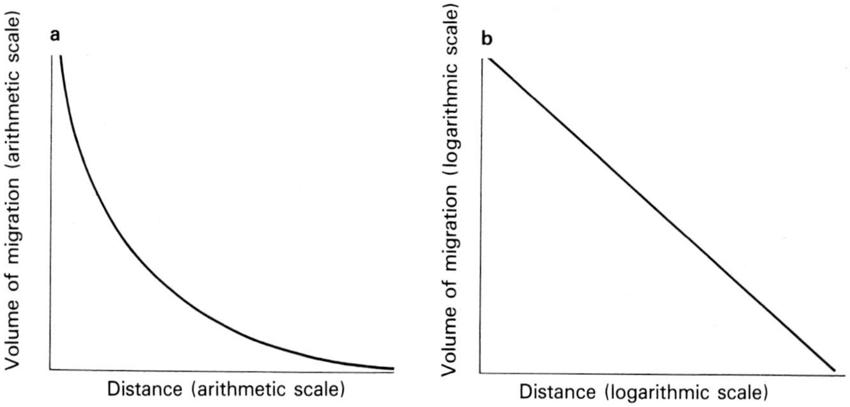

Figure 4.9 *The distance-decay relationship between volume of migration and distance:* **(a)** *arithmetic scales* **(b)** *logarithmic scales*

number of opportunities between the place of departure and the place of destination. The first part of the theory is consistent with the push-pull theory in that the opportunities at the destination are simply part of the pull force. Indeed, another of Ravenstein's original laws stated that migration increases in volume as industries and commerce develop and transport improves. Clearly implied here is the idea of increasing opportunities. The second part about intervening opportunities sees these as exercising a sort of frictional drag, reducing the volume of migration. Those opportunities can take many different forms: jobs, housing, good services, attractive amenities, etc.; they are things which persuade migrants to settle down 'en route' rather than complete the originally intended migration journey.

Stepwise migration

Stouffer's theory of intervening opportunities fits quite well with yet another of Ravenstein's

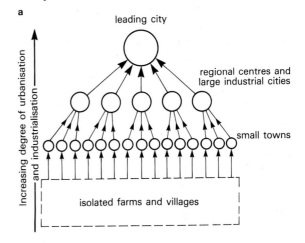

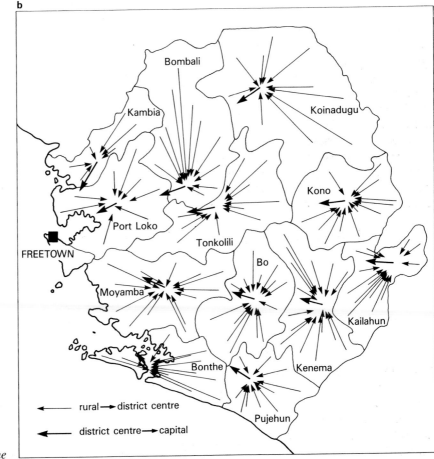

Figure 4.10 *Stepwise migration:*
(a) *hierarchical stepwise movement*
(b) *idealised migration flows in Sierra Leone*

laws, that 'migration occurs in stages and with a wave-like motion'. This is based on the observation made in the late nineteenth and early-twentieth centuries that migration tends to take place in a step-by-step manner up the settlement hierarchy. Crudely put, the capital or largest city draws migrants from other cities; in their turn, these draw people from towns in order to replace those who have moved to the capital; the towns then draw migrants from villages and rural areas to replace those who have moved on to cities. Thus migration to the leading city creates a sort of ripple or wave-like effect which eventually reaches out to the most remote parts of the country. As far as an individual migrant is concerned, a migration journey (for example from village to capital) is undertaken in this stepwise hierarchic way. Of course, at any one of those intervening stages, the perceived opportunities may be so great as to persuade the migrant to halt there, rather than complete the hierarchic progression. Figure 4.10a provides a simple model of stepwise migration. Figure 4.10b shows an idealised example from Sierra Leone, where migrants move from rural areas to district centres, and from there to Freetown, the largest settlement and capital city.

Two of Ravenstein's lesser known laws might just be cited here as being broadly relevant to the theme of the structure and direction of migration. The one stated that 'the major direction of migration is from agricultural areas to centres of industry and commerce'; the other that 'large towns grow more by migration than by natural increase'.

The selectivity of migration.

Ravenstein formulated three laws which recognised that the process of migration is inherently selective: that 'most migrants are adult and families rarely migrate out of their country of birth'; that 'women are more migratory than men within their country of birth, but men more frequently venture beyond it'; that 'town dwellers are less migratory than country dwellers'. These are three possible instances of

what is known as *differential migration*. The basic point is that under certain conditions and at certain times, some people and groups of people are more likely to migrate than others.

Particularly significant factors in differential migration are age, sex, education and occupation. For example, in many countries, young adults appear to be most migratory. Consider the age-pyramids of two locations in Guinea, Africa (Fig. 4.11). The city of Conakry on the coast has attracted people from the interior, especially from the over-populated Futa Jalon highlands. The population of Conakry appears to be dominated by young adults between the ages of 15 and 35; the dominant age groups in the highlands are 0 to 5 and 5 to 15. The implied high mobility of young adults is partly explained by a lack of family commitments in their area of birth; youthful ambition and economic motives also play a part. In advanced countries, retirement at the age of 60 or 65 provides the opportunity to move to a new residential location. Figure 4.12 shows the highest out-migration of elderly people from Greater London and the Outer Metropolitan Area towards the Outer South East, the South West and East Anglia, and lesser movements away from some provincial cities.

Age group	Conakry	Futa Jalon
	(males per 100 females)	
Under 15	87	95
15–45	126	62
Over 45	159	90

Table 4.3 *Sex ratios recorded at two locations in Guinea*

Sex selectivity appears to depend on the level of development in the country or region concerned. In advanced countries today, women are disproportionately more involved in short-distance migration and men more in long-distance migration. In the Third World, however, men constitute the majority in all migration streams, short- or long-distance, national or international. This is partly confirmed by the population pyramid for

Figure 4.11 *Age-sex pyramids for:*
(a) *Conakry*
(b) *Futa Jalon, Guinea*

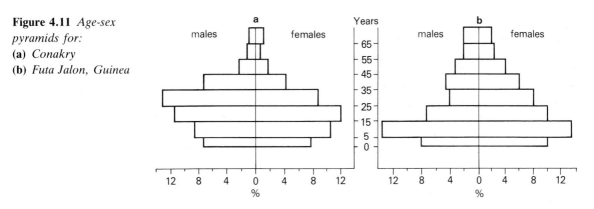

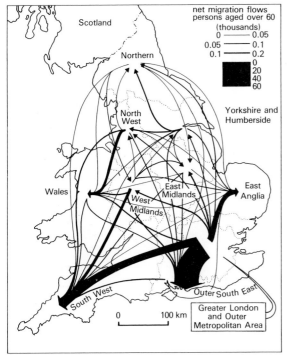

Figure 4.12 *Net inter-regional flows of those aged 60 or over, England and Wales (1961–1966)*

Conakry, except that in the 15 to 25 age group women slightly outnumber men (Fig. 4.11a). However, the more aggregate view of the two populations given in Table 4.3 shows how unbalanced the sex ratios have become as a result of the migration of males over the age of 15. Such sex selectivity is probably related, to some degree, to the prevalence of the traditional society. Because food production and child-rearing are still held to be women's work,

this creates the opportunity for men to seek alternative (often urban) work, and perhaps even the chance of higher education.

Education is a dual factor in the present context. Education beyond the statutory minimum school-leaving age often involves moving away from home to a distant college or university. Educational attainment frequently has a direct bearing on the type of occupation and possibly, therefore, ultimately on mobility. Empirical evidence shows professional people to be relatively more migratory than skilled and unskilled workers. Further, an investigation in the USA has shown, with respect to Stouffer's intervening opportunities model, that people in low-status jobs found proportionately more opportunities within a given distance than people in high-status jobs.

ASSIGNMENTS

8 Suggest explanations for, and comment critically on, the following of Ravenstein's laws:
   a. women are more migratory within their country of birth
   b. the natives of towns are less migratory than those of rural areas
   c. large towns grow· more by migration than natural increase.

9 Why is it that employees in low-status jobs are likely to find more intervening opportunities than people employed in high-status jobs?

10 Summarise and explain the pattern of migration flows shown by Figure 4.12.

MIGRATION POLICIES

Governments can exercise considerable influence in the context of migration; they can, and do, operate migration policies. Such intervention is a contentious issue, often giving rise to highly-charged and polarised feelings. On the one hand, it is argued that migration policies, particularly those which discourage movement, are an assault on the freedom of the individual. On the other hand, intervention tends to be justified on pragmatic grounds, along the lines that it is something done for the common good.

Policies of dissuasion

At an international level, policies may be either discouraging or encouraging, and apply either at the origin or the destination of a potential migration. These two criteria allow us, therefore, to construct a simple, fourfold classification of migration policies: dissuasion at the point of departure and the destination; encouragement at the destination and the point of departure.

The policies operated by the Soviet Union and the Eastern bloc provide good illustrations of those that have discouraged at the potential origin. The Berlin Wall and the virtually impregnable boundary fence constructed by East Germany along its frontier with West Germany symbolised a ruthless policy that up until 1989 allowed few would-be emigrants (not even dissidents) to leave for the West (Fig. 4.13). Equally, those same countries pursued policies which discouraged entry. The Iron Curtain was, in effect, a two-way barrier.

The United Kingdom also belongs to this second category in that it has put into effect policies designed to limit immigration. Those policies had their roots in the early post-war period. The 1948 British Nationality Act gave the citizens of the then British colonies and Commonwealth countries the right to enter, work and settle in Britain. Soon afterwards, the economic revival of Britain created an increased demand for labour; poverty and unemployment were rife in India, Pakistan and the countries of the Caribbean (Fig. 4.6, p. 81). This contained

Figure 4.13 *The Berlin Wall*
The Berlin Wall, first erected in 1961, stood for nearly 30 years not just as a symbol of a Germany divided between two political blocs. It was the material expression of the unilateral decision to obstruct migration and circulation between East and West. In these days of glasnost and perestroika, it is interesting to speculate for how much longer there will be political impediments to mobility within Europe.

situation encouraged a growing volume of immigration from the so-called *New Commonwealth* countries. Rising numbers of immigrants, combined with relatively high rates of natural increase, steadily increased the percentage importance of such immigrants in the British population (Table 4.4).

Year	Resident		Migrant (000s)		
	000s	**% total pop.**	**In**	**Out**	**Balance**
1951	218	0.4	38	39	−1
1956	est. 329	est. 0.7	33	24	+9
1961	541	1.1	44	20	+22
1966	973	1.8	77	42	+35
1971	1371	2.5	65	39	+26
1976	1771	3.3	67	30	+37
1981	2104	3.9	56	29	+27
1986	2432	4.4	34	13	+21

Table 4.4 *New Commonwealth and Pakistani immigrants in Great Britain*

Since 1962 a sequence of British Acts of Parliament has endeavoured to limit this migration stream. Understandably, the legislation has been severely criticised for being selective and discriminating against New Commonwealth immigrants. It is also held to be inhibiting immigrants already here from being joined by their relatives. The official justification given for the current policy is rooted in the poor housing, unemployment and poverty that are experienced by many first- and second-generation immigrants. There can be no doubt that a disproportionate number of the nearly 2.5 million residents of New Commonwealth origin are disadvantaged. Furthermore, the prevailing high levels of unemployment at a national level, together with riots in Bristol, Liverpool and London, possibly lend weight to the argument to restrict further immigration.

The United Kingdom is not alone in changing its stance on immigration. France was very keen, in the wake of two world wars, to recruit foreigners in order to make good the loss of its own young men and to provide much-needed manpower. Over six million immigrants, drawn from Poland, Southern Europe and North Africa, have been welcomed into France since 1920. These migrants have, in fact, been an important part of a much wider network of labour movements criss-crossing Europe (Fig. 4.14) from labour-surplus countries, such as Ireland, Spain, Italy, Greece and Turkey, to labour-hungry countries, such as France, West Germany and England. But the welcome in the latter countries lasted only up until the early 1970s. Since then, as in the United Kingdom, recession and racial tensions have rather changed the tone of official policy.

The open door?

It is tempting to think that the USA has actively pursued policies encouraging immi-

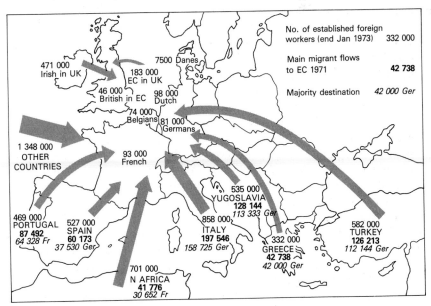

Figure 4.14 *Labour movements in the European Community (1973)*

Figure 4.15 *Emigration to the USA (1831–1910)*

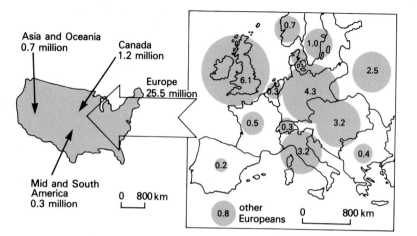

gration, and belongs therefore to the third category. It has received large numbers of European migrants over the last two centuries (Fig. 4.15). However, no such policies have ever existed, in that no tangible incentives were ever offered, other than an open door. Once there, a certain amount of encouragement was given to those nineteenth-century migrants to join in the westwards push of the pioneer frontier. But since 1907, when it feared 'yellow infiltration', the USA has employed increasingly restrictive measures to control the volume and quality of immigration. Here, as elsewhere, the tightening up has generated a backlash of illegal immigration, particularly in this case from Cuba and across the Mexican border. It is anyone's guess how many illegal aliens are now living in the United States or, for that matter, in the United Kingdom.

Australia is an interesting, contrasting case. The general policy since the late-eighteenth century has been to encourage immigration; people were needed to settle and develop the country. Up to 1939, Australia received about 2.5 million immigrants, of whom about a half benefited from government assistance which basically met the costs of removal. It would seem that Australia was operating an overtly encouraging policy. In reality, the policy has been selective, restricting the entry of certain types of people, excluding criminals (a little ironic bearing in mind the colonial origins of Australia!), the poor and the sick. Most no-

tably, it has debarred certain ethnic groups. The so-called *White Australia Policy* was justified on the grounds that Australia wished to preserve its European culture, and prevent an uncontrolled in-flow of Asian migrants.

Before 1939, Britons accounted for about 95 per cent of the assisted immigrants. After 1945, in order to speed up population growth and development, the Australian Government decided to raise the rate of immigration. The United Kingdom could no longer maintain the same percentage contribution and the Australian Government was persuaded to enter into migration agreements with other countries; in this event increasing numbers of migrants have been drawn from Western and Southern Europe and even Asia (Table 4.5). So it might seem that Australia has moved in the opposite direction to the UK and the USA in that there is now less discrimination on the basis of race and nationality. However, nowadays, entry visas are issued only to those who have skills that the country needs. So Australia has, in effect, toughened up on immigration by operating more stringent controls; in this respect, it is only doing what most countries have already done. The net effect, of course, is to make it more difficult for would-be emigrants to realise their ambitions.

Examples of the fourth and last category of migration policy are harder to find. It is not good for the image of a country, in the eyes of the international community, to be seen to be

Table 4.5 *The composition of immigration in Australia*

Origin	Arrivals of assisted immigrants (1947–72)	Birthplace (% of all population born overseas) (1986)		
Austria	21 972	Africa		3.3
Belgium	3 100	N America		3.6
W Germany	94 783	Asia		16.5
Greece	71 221	Europe		68.4
Italy	61 176	British Isles	34.7	
Malta	42 644	Germany	3.6	
Netherlands	81 258	Greece	4.2	
Spain	12 127	Italy	8.1	
Turkey	10 747	Yugoslavia	4.6	
UK	1 036 265	Other	13.2	
Yugoslavia	9 988	New Zealands		6.5
		Other		1.7
Refugees	257 652			
Others	162 195	TOTAL BORN OVERSEAS 3 247 381		
TOTAL	1 865 128	= 28.3% of total population		

deliberately pushing people out. For this reason, such policies tend to be unstated and discrete. But there are a few blatant examples, such as the displacement of the Jews from Germany during the 1930s and the expulsion of Asians from Uganda in the 1970s. Happily, such draconian practices are relatively rare, but there have been instances where the 'export' of people has been encouraged. There was little attempt to stop the mass movement of Irish people to Britain and to North America, despite the serious depopulation problems that ensued (Table 4.6). Between 1841 and 1951, the population declined by over one half. By 1861, there were already 1.6 million Irish-born in the United States, 800 000 in Britain and 286 000 in Canada; whilst between 1881 and 1971 net emigration from Ireland was 2.6 million. Since the 1970s, there has been a change in the nature of the migration balance.

Other examples of the fourth category include the persistent emigration from China, particularly to various parts of South East Asia. This has not been resisted, principally because it was in China's interests to shed some population. Similarly, the exodus of the 'boat people' from Vietnam, since it was overrun by the Communists in 1975, has not been dis-

Year	Total	% Change	Estimated net migration
1841	6 528 799	–	
1851	5 111 557	– 21.7	
1861	4 402 111	– 13.9	
1871	4 053 187	– 7.9	
1881	3 870 020	– 4.5	
1891	3 468 694	– 10.3	– 597 325
1901	3 221 823	– 7.1	– 396 414
1911	3 139 688	– 2.6	– 261 539
1926	2 971 992	– 5.6	– 405 029
1936	2 968 420	– 0.1	– 166 751
1946	2 898 264	– 2.4	– 187 111
1951	2 818 341	– 2.8	– 119 568
1961	2 884 002	+ 2.3	– 408 766
1971	2 978 248	+ 3.3	– 134 511
1981	3 443 405	+ 15.6	+ 103 889

Table 4.6 *The population of Ireland (1841–1981)*

couraged; again because it has been in the national interest (Fig. 4.16). After all, it has meant losing people unsympathetic to the new regimes and the war-ravaged economy has had fewer mouths to feed.

Internal policies

Migration policies can operate at a regional

Figure 4.16 *Flows of Vietnamese refugees in SE Asia (1975–1979)*

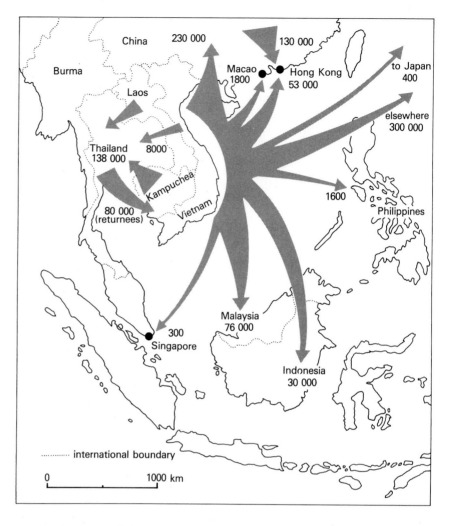

level within individual countries. This certainly applies to the planned economies of the Second World. The Soviet Union has endeavoured to bring about a redistribution of labour and to reduce the labour shortages in Siberia and the far north. Higher wages, cheaper housing and political promotion have been offered as inducements. The system of police registration and the issuing of work permits have also brought pressure to bear on those people with the special skills needed in the peripheral areas. The drafting of people to labour camps represents an even firmer way of implementing the policy.

Regional migration policies are not the exclusive preserve of the Communist bloc.

There is scarcely a country in the world today that is not seeking to redistribute people. Since 1945, under the guise of regional development programmes, Britain has pursued policies of persuading people to move out of London and other leading cities, either to nearby new towns and expanded towns or further afield to *assisted areas* (Fig. 4.17). In one respect, it might appear that this overspill policy has been too successful. There is talk now of 'overkill by overspill', as new devices, such as the *enterprise zone*, are being used to tempt people (and employment) back into the abandoned inner areas of Britain's major cities.

In a rather different context, the Israeli Government, which has been very active in

Figure 4.17 *Assisted Areas in Great Britain*

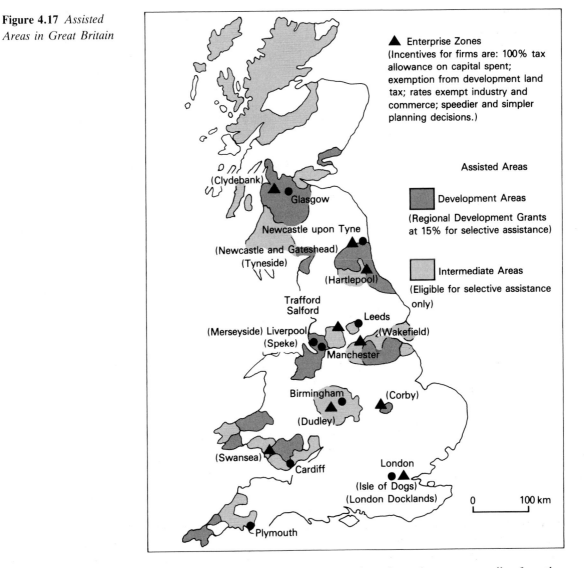

▲ Enterprise Zones
(Incentives for firms are: 100% tax allowance on capital spent; exemption from development land tax; rates exempt industry and commerce; speedier and simpler planning decisions.)

Assisted Areas

■ Development Areas
(Regional Development Grants at 15% for selective assistance)

□ Intermediate Areas
(Eligible for selective assistance only)

(Clydebank)
Glasgow
Newcastle upon Tyne
(Newcastle and Gateshead)
(Tyneside)
(Hartlepool)
Trafford
Salford
Leeds
(Merseyside) Liverpool (Wakefield)
(Speke)
Manchester
Birmingham (Corby)
(Dudley)
(Swansea)
Cardiff
London
(Isle of Dogs)
(London Docklands)
Plymouth

0   100 km

encouraging Jewish immigration, has also sought (for political and economic reasons) to encourage settlers to move to the annexed areas of the West Bank and the Gaza Strip, as well as to new settlements in the south of the country (Fig. 1.15, p. 26). At least it may be said of these, and many other regional migration policies in different parts of the world, that they do allow the individual a degree of choice. Such policies are not generating forced migration. Nonetheless, we must recognise that these policies, like those that apply to international migration, have been implemented for the na-tional good rather than necessarily for the benefit of the migrants themselves.

ASSIGNMENTS

11 Discuss the possible reasons for the Soviet Union's restrictive policies on international migration outside the Second World.
12 Analyse the data in either Table 4.4 or Table 4.6 by means of appropriate diagrams.
13 With reference to Table 4.5, analyse the changing composition of Australian immigration.
14 Suggest reasons for the particular pattern of

migration flows shown in either Figure 4.15 or Figure 4.16.

15 Debate the pros and cons of government intervention in migration.

16 Discuss the regional migration policies of one country, paying particular attention to the reasons behind, and the mechanisms of those policies.

ZELINSKY'S MOBILITY TRANSITION

So far, our examination of the causes and characteristics of migration has involved a rather static view of mobility. However, mobility, by definition, is a dynamic phenomenon in the two dimensions of space and time. Recent history reveals definite regularities in the way in which mobility has changed in different parts of the world, to the extent that it has become possible to recognise a series of stages. Zelinsky (1971) has made an important contribution here in defining that sequence of stages in what he calls the *mobility transition*. He argues that as a nation or region progresses through the various stages, there are orderly changes in both the type and the amount of spatial mobility, as well as changes in the types of migrant. The general transition is from very limited geographical and social mobility towards much wider and more elaborate forms of movement. The mobility transition comprises five phases which conveniently coincide with the demographic transition examined in Chapter 3. Zelinsky monitored progress through the transition by five different types of movement: international migration, frontierward migration, rural-urban migration, inter- and intra-urban migration, and circulation (Fig. 4.18a to e). The model also uses two other monitors, potential migration absorbed by circulation and potential circulation absorbed by communication systems (Fig. 4.18g and h); these will be explained shortly, as will the reasons for introducing a sixth type of movement, urban-rural, into the model (Fig. 4.18f).

Phase 1: The pre-modern industrial society

There is little migration during this stage, which is characterised by high rates of fertility and mortality and therefore by low rates of natural increase. The demographic character of the phase is essentially static. What little mobility there is tends to be mainly circulation associated with traditional subsistence practices, such as hunting and food gathering, shifting cultivation and nomadism (Fig. 4.18). Trading, social visits, tribal warfare and religious occasions also make a small contribution to mobility. There are few areas and peoples in the world today still at Phase 1; possible qualifiers include the fast-disappearing Inuit Indians of the Canadian Northlands and Greenland, the Amerindians of Amazonia, and the nomads of Somalia.

Phase 2: The early transitional society

A combination of a slight rise in fertility and a marked decline in mortality rates results in a higher rate of natural increase. The need to feed an increasing total population encourages people to colonise new areas for agricultural use. Thus there takes place what Zelinsky calls *frontierward* migration into more remote and hitherto unused parts of the country (Fig. 4.18b). This is well illustrated by the advance of settlement in Brazil during the colonial period (Fig. 4.19). Also at this time, there is a growing volume of rural-urban migration stimulated by economic development and its associated urbanisation. As people generally become more mobile and freed from the tasks of food production, they might even be tempted by opportunities in other countries to emigrate. In the other direction, the prospects of further economic development and of resource exploitation might tempt an immigration of skilled workers, businessmen, technicians and professional people from more advanced parts of the world. During this phase, there is also significant growth in various kinds of circulation. Much of this relates to the growing towns and includes: the periodic movements of rural people travelling to towns for goods and

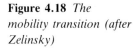

Figure 4.18 *The mobility transition (after Zelinsky)*

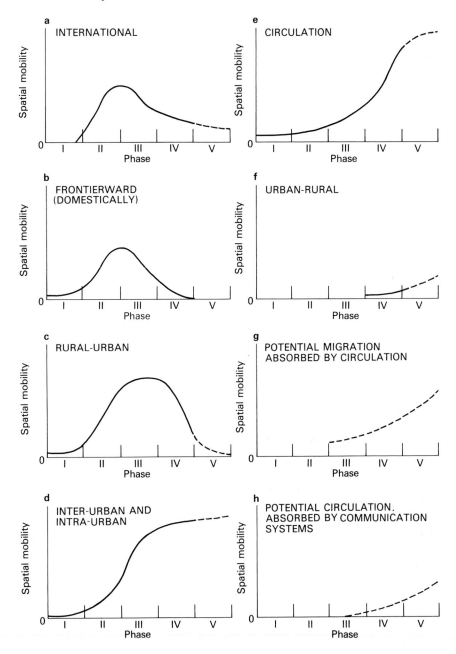

services; visits between relatives now living on either side of the rural-urban divide, and labour circulation associated with the availability of seasonal work.

Phase 3: The late transitional society

The rate of natural increase declines, princi-

pally due to a major fall in the fertility rate. Frontierward migration begins to decline as colonisation gradually spreads to virtually all parts of the national territory; the stock of unused land becomes exhausted (Fig. 4.18b). Thus rural-urban migration becomes the dominant movement, but the rate begins to slacken as the labour needs of towns and cities

Figure 4.21 *The spread of London's Jewish population*

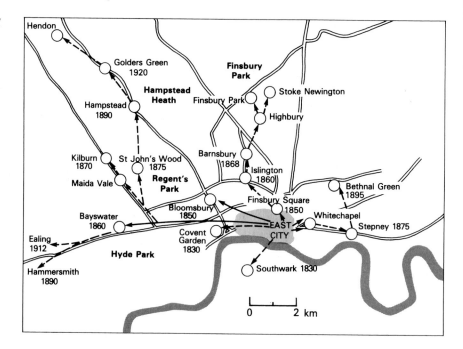

considerable growth in the volume of commuting from new suburbs increasingly distant from city and town centres.

Phase 5: A future super-advanced society

Zelinsky published his mobility transition model in 1971 and much has happened since then as regards the global economic climate, social change and technological progress. Hindsight allows us to comment on the realism or otherwise of the predictions he made for the fifth phase (Fig. 4.18, p. 95). It is early days yet, but experience so far in the *sunbelt regions* of advanced countries (for example, southern California, metropolitan Tokyo and Britain's M4 corridor) suggests that he was right in thinking that advances in communications technology would reduce the need for some forms of circulation, particularly in the world of business and commerce. This is what Zelinsky meant in Figure 4.18h by 'potential circulation absorbed by communication systems.' On the other hand, transport improvements, trends in the pattern of urbanisation, and social changes are certainly helping to sustain the level of circulation. For example, they are contributing

to more and even longer-distance commuting, to a growing volume of weekly movements connected with out-of-town shopping, and to more tourism and pleasure trips. In addition, there are developments anticipated by the graph entitled 'potential migration absorbed by circulation' (Fig. 4.18g). In other words, movements that formerly required a change of permanent residence might now be undertaken without any such change. For example, a second home in Wales, somewhere close to the M4 motorway, allows the London-based businessman to enjoy rural life, albeit only at weekends and holiday times (Fig. 4.22).

Recent events suggest that Zelinsky's prediction that nearly all migration will be of the inter-urban and intra-urban variety needs some qualification. Certainly, there seems to be no reduction in intra-urban movement, particularly from inner city to suburb. But what is becoming increasingly apparent is that the largest cities are shedding population and that the highest rates of growth are now being experienced by freestanding low- and middle-order cities. In other words, the onset of *decentralisation* is beginning to reverse stepwise migration up the urban hierarchy. Then there is the growing

Figure 4.22 *A second home in Gwynedd, Wales*
Rising affluence, improved personal mobility and the wish to spend leisure time outside the city, have led to increasing numbers of rural dwellings being bought by Western urbanites as second homes. The part-time occupation of country properties, at weekends and during holidays, sometimes generates strong local resentment. This particular second home has been the victim of an arson attack, an extreme expression of that opposition.

strength of what is called *counterurbanisation*, namely the increasing movement of people (both economically-active and retired) from city to countryside. This strengthening process is well shown by the migrational shifts which occurred in England and Wales between 1971 and 1981 (Fig. 4.23). It represents a profound reversal of migration direction, perhaps stimulated by a growing disillusionment with city living and a wish for a calmer, simpler and safer life style. Certainly the costs and benefits of rural living as compared with urbanism are currently undergoing a basic reassessment, and there is every expectation of a growing tide of urban-rural migration. For this reason, it has been

added to Zelinsky's model (Fig. 4.18f, p. 95).

One aspect of the model needs to be made clear, namely that countries have progressed along the transition at different rates. It is necessary to allow for a variable time scale, and, as with the demographic transition, it does appear that late starters tend to make more rapid progress. For example, it took England and Wales some 200 years to complete the graduation from Phase 2 to Phase 4, whilst it has taken Japan about a quarter of that time. Equally, both the migration and demographic transition models are based on the experiences of developed countries. The question inevitably arises, can the developing countries of the

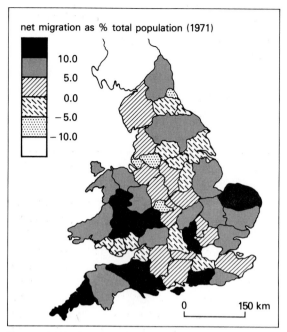

net migration as % total population (1971)

10.0
5.0
0.0
−5.0
−10.0

0   150 km

Figure 4.23 *Migration balances in England and Wales, by county (1971–1981)*

world today necessarily expect to follow exactly the same transitional paths?

ASSIGNMENTS

17 Suggest some more ways in which:
   a. potential migration is being absorbed by circulation
   b. potential circulation is being absorbed by communication systems.

18 What factors might be expected to alter the mobility transition followed by today's developing countries?

19 Compare the migration patterns shown by Figures 4.20 and 4.23.

20 With reference to Figure 4.21, suggest reasons for the movement of the Jewish population within London.

21 Correlate Zelinsky's mobility transition with the demographic transition model discussed in Chapter 3.

22 With reference to Figure 4.22, discuss the pros and cons of people buying second homes in rural areas.

THE CONSEQUENCES OF MIGRATION

Just as each population movement has its causes, so each migration and circulation has its consequences, both for the area of origin and the area of destination. Many of those consequences fall into the same descriptive categories recognised in connection with the causes of mobility (economic, environmental, social and political), but it is necessary to define two more – demographic and cultural. These six categories will provide the structure for the following discussion. The illustrative material will be drawn mainly from international migration and from the various types of mobility associated with urbanisation. International migration is renowned for its diversity, volume and distance; the process of urbanisation has generated its own types of movement which are no less impressive as regards their scale and impact upon modern society. Figure 4.24 indicates the four main directions of migration created by urbanisation – rural-urban, inter-urban, intra-urban and urban-rural.

Increased circulation in advanced countries

Although this section is about the consequences of migration, it should be mentioned that a whole range of different circulations may also be attributed to urbanisation. In most advanced countries, the volume of circulation has increased enormously over the last few decades. Major contributors to this increase include improved transport, greater personal mobility and changing residential preferences. These have given rise to a decentralisation of population, rippling out from inner city to outer suburb, from city to dormitory town, from town to countryside. But the distribution of employment opportunities has not changed to the same degree. As a consequence, there is an increased spatial dislocation of home and work, and more and more people commute, many over longer distances. In the case of London, for example, recent improvements to the mainline railway

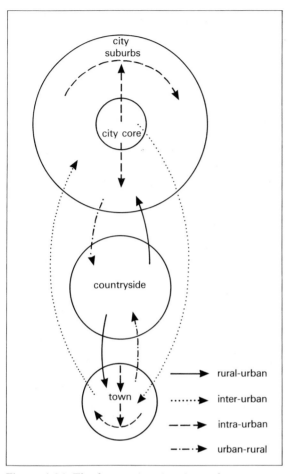

Purpose	% of all journeys
Commuting	25
In course of work	2
Education	8
Shopping	19
Personal business	13
Social and entertainment	26
Holiday, day trips	5
Other	2

Table 4.7 *Journey purpose in Great Britain (1985)*

Figure 4.24 *The four main migrations of urbanisation*

Legend in figure:
— rural–urban
⋯⋯⋯ inter–urban
– – – intra–urban
–·–·– urban–rural

frequently overloaded infrastructure creates consequential costs, such as noise, pollution, congestion and accidents. Increased circulation at an international level, particularly in the context of tourism, is also having far-reaching repercussions. These may range from congestion of airports and airways at peak holiday times to the congestion of once beautiful coastlines by sunbathers, modern hotels and tourist trappings; not to mention the profound impact on the traditional economies and societies of *honeypot* areas such as the Costa Brava, Majorca and Florida (Fig. 4.25).

Demographic effects

The most obvious outcome of migration is a redistribution of population. The reciprocal movement between two areas will usually be unequal; one area gains and the other loses population. The impact of migration on the distribution of population is perhaps most strikingly seen in areas undergoing pioneer settlement and development, as in the opening up of North America and Australia by European settlers. But the same process has also taken place relatively recently in Europe itself, as people have moved to peripheral areas characterised by rather harsh environments. For example, the higher rates of population growth in northern Sweden during the nineteenth century, shown by Figure 4.26, were largely the product of migration. As people moved northwards, so there was some reduction in the acute concentration of the Swedish population in the southern half of the country. On the other

system have led to people commuting from as far afield as Norwich, Doncaster, Bristol and Bournemouth. Whilst commuting is undoubtedly the major contributor to the growth in circulation, it is not the only one. Increased levels of affluence, wider car-ownership and shorter working hours have led to higher levels of trip generation in connection with weekly shopping (perhaps at some out-of-town hypermarket rather than in the CBD), recreation and leisure (Table 4.7).

The irony of all this increased circulation is that its major consequence is to make even greater demands on the very thing that appears to have generated it in the first place – the transport infrastructure. Increased use of that

Figure 5.4 *Death on the battlefield, 1917*
During the First World War (1914–18), nearly 10 million military personnel (mainly men) were killed. For the Second World War (1939–45), the figure was 15.6 million, but in addition to these casualties, it is known that over 39 million civilians lost their lives. Clearly, such immense fatalities had profound demographic consequences which included not just heightened levels of mortality, but the lowering of birth rates and the fundamental reshaping of age-sex pyramids.

selective (see p. 103), can also have a dual impact. In areas of net migration loss, the pyramid will become eroded; in areas of net gain there will be aggradation.

When analysing the age-structure of a population, three fundamental distinctions are drawn; these are between *children and adolescents, adults* and *the elderly*. There is no universal agreement as to the precise age thresholds to be used in defining these three groups. Probably the most widely used are either 15 or 20 years for the boundary between

the first and second, and 65 years for the second and third. The practical significance of these groups, within a given population, lies in the contexts of economic support and the provision of particular types of services. In terms of economic support, it is clear that the adult population (15 or 20 to 65) is the productive or *active* element of the population – the employed people who constitute the breadwinners. The other two groups tend to be economically inactive and therefore *dependent* on working adults. The *dependency ratio* is a simple

Figure 5.5 *A baby clinic in Southampton*
Not only are baby booms often difficult to forecast (as was the British boom in the 1960s), they can create a whole range of problems. One of these is the short-term need to make available sufficient ante- and post-natal services for the temporary increase in expectant mothers and young children. If adequate provision has been made, there is the inevitability that, once the boom has passed, there will an excess and underused service capacity.

measure of that reliance, derived by using the formula:

$$D = 100 \, \frac{x + y}{p}$$

where x is the population under 15 or 20 years, y the population of 65 years and over, and p the population aged between 15 (or 20) and 64. The ratio purports to measure approximately how many dependents every 100 people in the productive group must support. The approxi-

mation reflects the fact that not all men and women in the 15 to 64 age-range will be employed. Quite a lot of teenagers will stay on at school after the minimum leaving age, and those who go on to higher education will not become economically active until their early 20s. Many women leave active employment for a length of time to raise families, and not all may subsequently return to work. On the other hand, an increasing number of people of retirement age will continue to be economically active.

The dependency ratio is most valuable in an economic sense in that it indicates the burden of support that is likely to fall on the economically-active people. That burden is not only to provide dependents with food, clothing and housing. It also includes the provision of a range of services which are, in many cases, specific to the needs of each of the two groups of dependents – for example, schools for children and sheltered housing for the elderly. If the under-5 cohort greatly outnumbers the over-60 cohort, then this would suggest that public expenditure should give priority to the provision of educational facilities; the converse situation would call for greater expenditure on such things as geriatric wards, day-care centres, and 'meals-on-wheels' services. In addition, the proportional importance of young dependents at any one time gives an indication of the number of jobs that will have to be created in the near future when those dependents leave school. Similarly, the proportional size of the active population gives an indication of the scale of provision that will have to be made in the future when those people retire.

	Dependency ratio		
	Total	**Young** (< 15 yrs)	**Elderly** (> 64 yrs)
Africa	94	88	6
Asia	65	57	8
Europe	50	31	19
Latin America	70	65	5
North America	50	33	17
Oceania	56	43	13
USSR	52	38	14
World	65	55	10

Table 5.1 *Dependency ratios, by continent (1985)*

Table 5.1 shows that dependency ratios vary quite considerably between the major regions of the world. They are above the global average of 65 in Africa and Latin America; Asia is on the average; while Europe, North America, Oceania and the USSR are well below the average. The dependency load in Africa is approaching twice that in Europe. A further difference between these two groups is that the dependence in Africa overwhelmingly involves the young, whereas in Europe (although the young still constitute the majority) there is a much higher incidence of elderly dependents. This difference is, of course, a function of fertility and mortality rates; when high these increase the proportion of young dependents, and when low the proportion of elderly dependents is increased. The difference also implies a difference in population prospects, with growth inevitable in the African situation of a high incidence of young dependents who will soon reach the reproductive age-range. In Europe, with its greater proportion of people who have passed through that age-range, there is the distinct possibility of natural decrease.

The age pyramids for two contrasting countries, Ethiopia and the USA, are shown in Figure 5.6. The progressive pyramid of Ethiopia (Fig. 5.6a) indicates that nearly half the population is aged under 15. This is more than double the value in the regressive pyramid of the USA (Fig. 5.6d). In contrast, the percentage of the population aged 65 and over is three times greater in the USA. The age pyramids of both countries have been drawn twice, using age-group intervals of five and ten years. In the latter case (Fig. 5.6b and c), it is interesting to compare the percentage values for the populations aged under 20 and over 60, and to note the impact of the different age interval on the appearance of the age pyramids.

Figure 5.7 shows how the composition and relative importance of Britain's dependent population changed as the country passed through the demographic transition (1841–1981). The incidence of young people under the age of 15 years declined from 36 per cent to 21 per cent, the decline being most marked between 1891 and 1931. At the same time, the percentage importance of elderly people in the population more than quadrupled from 4 per cent to 17 per cent. Active adults now account for 62 per cent of the total population and the dependency ratio is therefore 61. Current forecasts suggest that by the year 2000, the elderly will constitute 20 per cent of the

Figure 5.6 *Age-sex pyramids for Ethiopia and the USA (1985)*

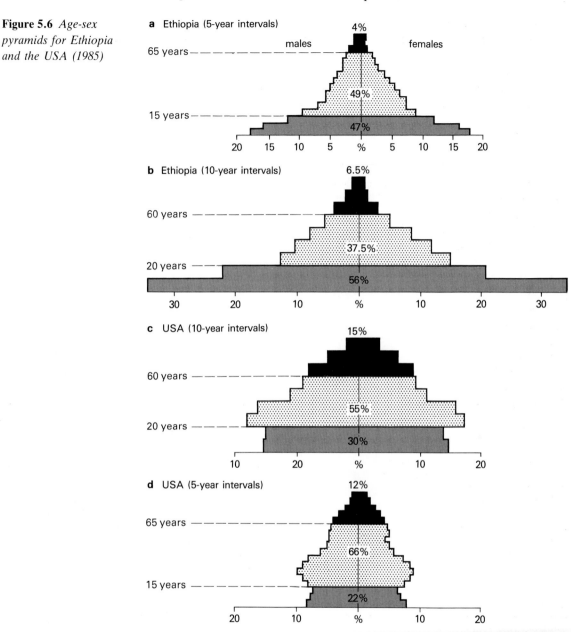

a Ethiopia (5-year intervals)

b Ethiopia (10-year intervals)

c USA (10-year intervals)

d USA (5-year intervals)

population; the same figure is forecast for the young. These figures imply a raising of the dependency ratio to 67. Figure 5.8 shows similar processes of change working their way through the age pyramid of Japan over a period of 90 years. Here the prognosis is that by the year 2040, 22 per cent of Japan's population will be aged 65 and over, and 18 per cent aged under 15 years.

These changes in the age-structure of the population so clearly illustrated in Great Britain and Japan create two sets of problems. On the one hand, there is the issue of what to do with those services which exist principally for the benefit of the young. Do we close down schools, maternity wards, post-natal clinics and children's libraries as numbers fall below the economic thresholds required to maintain those

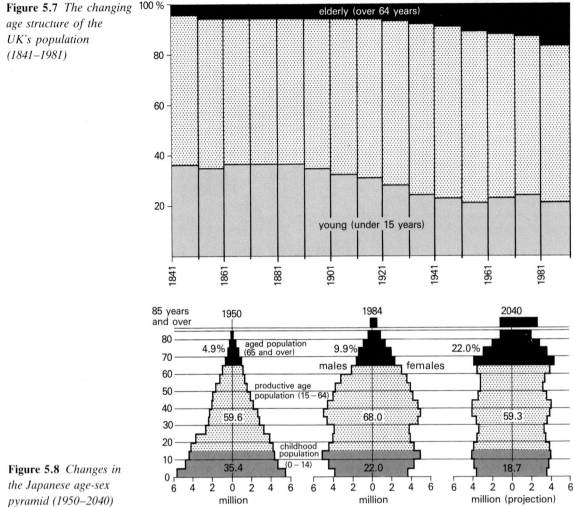

Figure 5.7 *The changing age structure of the UK's population (1841–1981)*

Figure 5.8 *Changes in the Japanese age-sex pyramid (1950–2040)*

services? Or are they to be maintained at a growing expense to the active population? At the same time, there is the challenge of making proper provision for the silvering population, providing state pensions, retirement housing and various types of social and welfare service geared to the needs of the elderly (Fig. 5.16, p. 127). Again, this might be seen as adding to the burden of support borne by the active population.

Sex ratios

Whilst the numbers of males and females in a population are broadly similar, there are some disparities which are of interest to geographers. The precise nature of the balance between the sexes is measured by the *sex ratio*. This is usually derived by calculating the number of males per 100 females; less commonly, males (or females) are expressed as a percentage of the total population.

Sex ratios are broadly influenced by three demographic factors which need brief discussion. First, there is the biological fact that male births exceed female births. This is not something unique to the human race; it is also experienced by most species of mammal. In the United Kingdom, for example, there are some 1053 males born to every 1000 females. Why

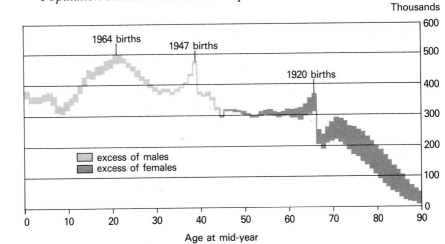

Figure 5.9 *The UK's population, by age and sex (1985)*

this should be is not readily explained. Research has shown that, in the human population, many more males are conceived than females, and that this excess is reduced, but not eliminated, by the greater incidence of male still-births. It has also been shown that the sex ratio at birth is directly related to the level of living and the standard of ante-natal hygiene and care. As these conditions improve, so the sex ratio at birth tends to increase. That general trend is well illustrated by the data for the United Kingdom given in Table 5.2. The drop in the ratio in 1930–32 may be explained by the relative privation accompanying the economic depression of that time. The relatively high ratios between 1950 and 1970 reflect postwar prosperity, whilst the recent towering might be related to current recession.

The second biological influence is the one discussed on p. 86; in most parts of the world male mortality rates are higher than female rates and, as a result, women enjoy longer life expectancy. Clearly, this helps to reduce the initial preponderance of males at birth. Also helping to reduce that superiority in numbers is the fact that the male population experiences higher rates of infant mortality (Table 5.3). The impact of these two biological factors is well shown in Figure 5.9. This analyses the United Kingdom's population by age and sex. It shows that, up to the age of 40, there is an excess of males; after that, the situation is one of an increasing surplus of females up to the age of 80, followed by an inevitable tapering down.

The third influence comes through migration. The point has been made on p. 86 that many migrations are sex-selective. In the past, men migrated more readily than women, contributing to higher sex ratios at their destinations

	Males born per 1000 females
1900–02	1037
1910–12	1039
1920–22	1052
1930–32	1046
1940–42	1062
1950–52	1061
1960–62	1063
1970–72	1064
1980–82	1053

Table 5.2 *Mean live-birth sex ratios in the UK (1900–1982)*

	Male	Female
	(per 1000 live births)	
Australia	11.2	9.0
Canada	8.7	7.1
Chile	20.8	18.1
France	9.5	7.1
Mexico	36.4	29.3
Sri Lanka	33.9	27.3
Tunisia	38.9	34.0

Table 5.3 *Infant mortality rates for selected countries (1985)*

and lower ratios in their areas of origin. Today, however, there appears to be less sex discrimination in the context of migration.

	Males per 100 females
Africa	99
Asia	105
Europe	95
Latin America	100
North America	95
Oceania	101
USSR	89
World	101

Table 5.4 *Sex ratios, by continent (1985)*

	Males per 100 females
1820	103.3
1830	103.1
1840	103.7
1850	104.3
1860	104.7
1870	102.2
1880	103.6
1890	105.0
1900	104.4
1910	106.0
1920	104.0
1930	102.5
1940	100.7
1950	98.6
1960	97.1
1970	94.8
1980	94.5

Table 5.5 *Sex ratios in the USA (1820–1980)*

Sex ratios vary spatially, as is illustrated by the data in Table 5.4. Broadly speaking, sex ratios in the USSR, Europe and North America are less than 100; they are particularly low in the USSR. In part, these low ratios reflect the fact that women in the developed world enjoy greater life expectancy than men. They also reflect the sex-selective impact of two World Wars, as well as the effects of emigration to the New World which has tended to be male-

dominated. This last factor also helps to explain the high sex ratios in the pioneer areas of countries such as Australia, Canada and the USA.

Table 5.5 shows how the male-surplus situation in the United States has been gradually eroded since about 1910, as total population growth has been derived increasingly from natural increase rather than net immigration. In other, and less developed, parts of the world today, sex ratios are often more than 100. For example, there are 4.2 million more males than females in Pakistan, 2.7 million more in Bangladesh, and 1 million more in Iraq. This phenomenon may be explained by the traditionally lower status of women and by the manifestation of that in higher rates of mortality. It is also exaggerated by the tendency for females to be under-enumerated in censuses.

Figure 5.10 is included to exemplify the point that sex ratios vary, not only between continents and countries, but also within nations. It shows that, within the UK, men are in shortest supply in Wales and in most abundance in the West Midlands, but even there the sex ratio is below 100.

It is difficult to attribute many direct consequences to unbalanced sex ratios. Tangible consequences are only likely to occur when and where the imbalance is considerable. One obvious effect is that monogamous family life is debarred from a significant proportion of those adults belonging to the numerically superior sex. This can result in an increased degree of deviant behaviour, particularly in the contexts of sexual relationships, recreation and community life. Some studies have suggested that, except in those societies which permit a man to have more than one wife, low sex ratios tend to depress fertility rates. Contrary to expectation, however, high sex ratios do not appear to reduce fertility (Table 4.9, p. 104). A degree of role reversal has been observed in some instances, whereby the occupations traditionally filled by persons of the sex in short supply are filled by persons of the sex in surplus. In contrast, it has also been shown in some rural areas suffering from out-migration

Figure 5.10 *Regional variations in sex ratios in the UK (1985)*

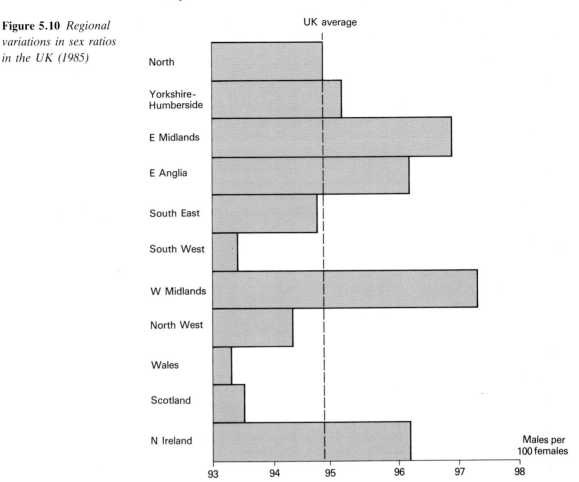

that the loss of males has had an adverse impact on farming. Equally, there are other parts of the world where food production is regarded as women's work and so the departure of men seeking work in towns and cities has no such consequence. However, one common consequence in urban centres with surplus males (particularly ports, mining and pioneer towns) is the relatively high incidence of prostitution.

Race

Any comments about the possible significance of race as an aspect of population structure have to be couched most carefully. For example, there is considerable statistical data from the USA which appears to indicate the existence of demographic differences between the white and black populations in terms of both fertility and mortality rates (see pp. 39–40 and pp. 40–45). However, it seems likely that these are explained by disparities in standards of living rather than by differences in physiology. Elsewhere, what appear to be racial divergences can frequently be explained by differences in ethnicity, particularly contrasts in attitude towards children and family life. For example, such comments may well apply to the differences between New Commonwealth and Pakistani immigrants and the indigenous population in Britain (Table 4.9, p. 104). Nonetheless, no matter what the causal mechanism, if particular racial groups can be identified as showing distinct demographic characteristics, then racial composition (the relative sizes of those groups within the multi-racial society) must be recognised as a significant dimension of population structure.

ASSIGNMENTS

---

1 With reference to Figures 5.2 and 5.6, assess the relative merits of using *one, five* and *ten-year* age-group intervals in the construction of age pyramids.
2 Explain the spatial variations in the dependency ratios shown in Table 5.1.
3 Plot the data in Table 5.5 on a graph. Suggest a full explanation for the overall trend shown on your graph.
4 Discuss possible reasons for the regional variations in sex ratios shown by Figure 5.10.
5 With reference to Figures 5.5 and 5.16, which do you think presents the greater difficulties in the context of service provision – a baby boom or an ageing population? Justify your viewpoint.

CULTURAL OR ETHNIC CHARACTERISTICS

Reference to race leads to consideration of the cultural or ethnic dimension of population structure. Different aspects of ethnicity – race, language, religion and nationality – provide a basis for distinguishing between people. Equally, they can and do provide a bond between people sharing the same ethnic attribute. This bonding tends to be particularly strong if the ethnic group happens to be a minority element in some larger population. The sense of being in some way different from the majority of the population often finds expression in residential segregation. Members of an ethnic group will often be found concentrated in particular locations. It may be helpful briefly to consider some examples before discussing the processes which give rise to this segregation.

Segregation

At the macro-scale, the recognition of ethnic

differences and the wish to formalise the segregation of different groups have, on occasions, led to the creation of new nations. The partition of the British Empire of India into India and West and East Pakistan (East Pakistan became Bangladesh in 1971) at the end of colonial rule in 1947 is a case in point. It reflected the occurrence of two main religious groups, the Hindus and Moslems, and the mutual desire of those groups to live apart in separate states (Fig. 5.11). At about the same time, the creation of Israel out of Palestine reflected, in part, the inherent antagonism between Jews and Arabs.

Religion still seems to be a particularly strong divider or spatial segregator of people, even within nations and between sects of the same religion. In Sri Lanka, the Tamils are a Hindu minority concentrated in the north of the island. In the second half of the 1980s, they pressured to be granted independence from the largely Buddhist Singalese. Cyprus is divided into Greek and Turkish sectors, the basis of the partition being a powerful mix of religion and nationalism. In Belgium, the Christian community is divided into Catholics and Protestants, with the former (the Walloons) mainly living in the south of the country, and the latter (the Flemish) concentrated in the north. Here the religious divide is reinforced by a linguistic difference; the Walloons speak French, whilst the Flemish speak Dutch. Northern Ireland suffers the same sectarianism, except that here it is reinforced by differences in nationalist aspirations. The wish of the minority Catholic community is that Ulster should join the Irish Republic; in contrast, the Protestants wish to remain part of the United Kingdom. The intensity of the feeling between the two communities has led to a highly localised segregation, which is well shown both within the Province as a whole and within Belfast in particular (Fig. 5.12).

The ghetto

Localised ethnic or cultural segregation is a characteristic of many cities. City populations

Figure 5.11 *The partition of India*

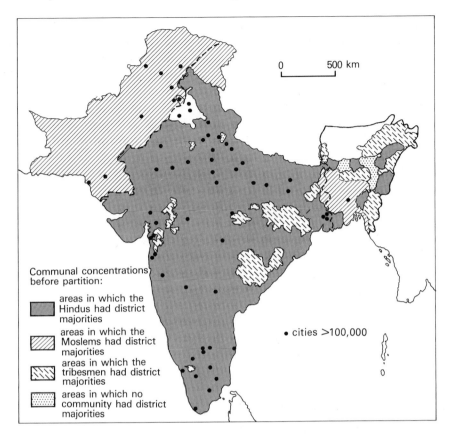

Communal concentrations before partition:

▨ areas in which the Hindus had district majorities

▨ areas in which the Moslems had district majorities

▨ areas in which the tribesmen had district majorities

▨ areas in which no community had district majorities

• cities >100,000

0 ——— 500 km

are typically cosmopolitan; the perceived opportunities of cities draw people from different directions and backgrounds. The term *ghetto* is commonly used to describe the concentration of a particular ethnic minority. Originally used to describe the Jewish quarters of European cities in the Middle Ages, it was subsequently adopted in the nineteenth century to denote the immigrant districts of North American cities, typically located in the *zone of transition* immediately outside the *central business district*. In this century, the term has been increasingly used in connection with the segregation of racial groups, particularly of non-white people. Because the people constituting a ghetto are often disadvantaged in some way or another, and because the ghetto frequently occupies an inner-city location, it is typically (but not always) an area of poor housing and low income.

Contemporary examples of ghettos are many and various. Reference has already been made in Chapter 4 to the cases of New York, with its concentrations of non-Whites (Fig. 4.30, p. 105) and of London, with its shifting Jewish ghetto (Fig. 4.21, p. 98) and its localisations of New Commonwealth and Pakistani immigrants (Fig. 4.29, p. 105). Other examples might include the Arab quarters of the larger cities in France; or, from the other side of the world, the concentrations of immigrants from Southern Europe in the poorer areas of Australian cities (Fig. 5.13); or the 'Chinatowns' to be found in cities all around the globe, from London to San Francisco, Melbourne to Yokohama. The modern ghetto is very much the product of international migration.

Explanations of the processes which give rise to the segregation of cultural or ethnic minorities vary. On the one hand, it may be seen as a spontaneous outcome reflecting the wishes of members of the group. For example, there is

Figure 5.12 *The distribution of Roman Catholics in:*
(a) *Ulster*
(b) *Belfast*

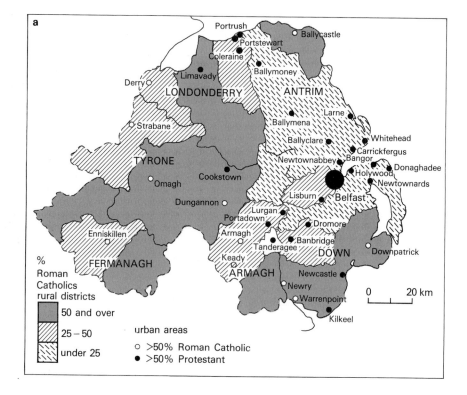

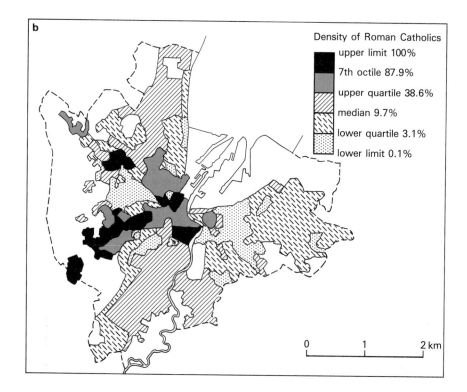

the psychological desire to live in close proximity to those of a similar background and tradition and the greater feeling of personal security that is to be derived from so doing. This may be particularly strong if the minority group happens to be readily visible by virtue of such things as skin colour or clothing. Living with other members of the group may also appeal if, as a result of concentration, the minority community is able to sustain the provision of services and amenities to meet its special needs. These might include a place of worship, a community centre, a school and food shops; in other words, things that will strengthen the group bond and help maintain the group identity.

In stark contrast to the general view that segregation is essentially a voluntary process, it may be argued that it is the product of discriminatory action by the *charter group* (the host population of an immigrant group) or by the majority community. Ethnic and cultural minorities are frequently denied access to anything but the most menial and poorest paid jobs. Low wages mean that they concentrate in areas of cheap and often substandard housing, and live at high densities. In such areas, the provision of health, educational and welfare services may be poor, another apparent aspect of discrimination. The argument proceeds that the outcome of all these things, together with the fact that the group is often small in number, is that it commands little political power, and

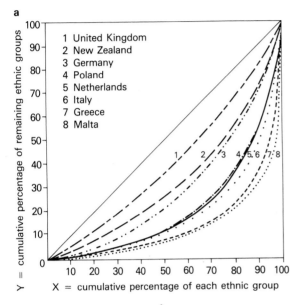

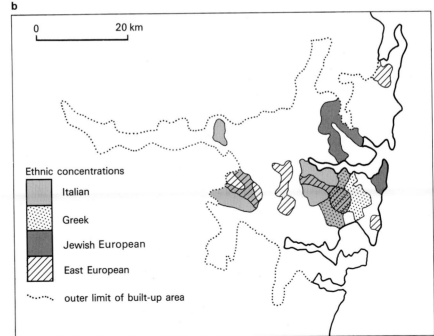

Figure 5.13 *Ethnic concentrations in:*
(a) *Melbourne*
(b) *Sydney*

can do little to reduce its own *multiple deprivation*.

The actual explanation probably involves elements of both these views of cultural or ethnic segregation, and clearly the nature of the explanation will vary with the particular circumstances. However, what can be agreed is this: once it has been formed, a ghetto does have a momentum of its own. Despite the fact that there may be *assimilation* and members of the group do move elsewhere, the ghetto will persist, although not always in exactly the same location. In the case of the ghetto functioning as the reception area for an in-migrating group, those leaving will most likely be replaced by others following along the same migration stream. In nearly all cases, it is likely to be the wish of a significant number of residents to remain where they are and to raise their families in the ghetto. The same is broadly true where segregation applies at a regional or national scale.

Therefore the prime interest of population geographers in the cultural or ethnic structure of populations lies in this recurrent tendency for different groups to become spatially segregated nationally, regionally and locally. There is, however, a second aspect which concerns the geographer. This is related to the fact that in many cases particular cultural groups may be distinguished by certain demographic attributes, particularly with respect to fertility, family size and contraception. Although death is a great leveller, there also appear to be some differences in the mortality rates of ethnic groups. Such differences are probably explained by the everyday living habits (especially the diet) that are an integral and often distinguishing cultural trait. These demographic associations were examined and illustrated on pp. 40 and 45. What they all mean is that spatial variations in certain vital aspects of population (particularly birth and death rates and therefore rates of population growth) may sometimes be explained by the distributions of certain cultural or ethnic groups and by their relative frequencies in the composition of a particular population.

ASSIGNMENTS

6 Which of the following ethnic attributes – race, language, nationality and religion – is the most significant in terms of population geography? Justify your choice.
7 With reference to one ghetto, assess the relative merits of the two opposing theories put forward to explain ghetto formation.
8 Explain and illustrate how culture may influence fertility and mortality rates.

SOCIO-ECONOMIC VARIABLES

This third category embraces quite a diversity of structural characteristics, ranging from marital to socio-economic status, from household size to place of residence. The examination of these variables will be both brief and selective. Most of the illustrative material will be drawn from Great Britain, and needs to be prefaced by two comments. First, the characteristics and trends observed in Britain are probably shared by many of those developed countries which have completed the demographic transition. Equally, there are probably many more countries where the characteristics and trends are substantially different. The attributes considered here, therefore, provide potential criteria for distinguishing between different parts of the world.

Marital status

The term *marital status*, in fact, embraces four different statuses – single (never-married), married, divorced and widowed. Clearly, marriage is the pivotal status in this fourfold scheme. Some population geographers regard marital status as a demographic rather than a socio-economic variable. Others see marriage as a legal and religious institution, rather than a biological phenomenon. It is something which is recognised and encouraged in many parts of the world in order to ensure group survival through child-bearing. In most societies,

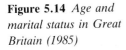

Figure 5.14 *Age and marital status in Great Britain (1985)*

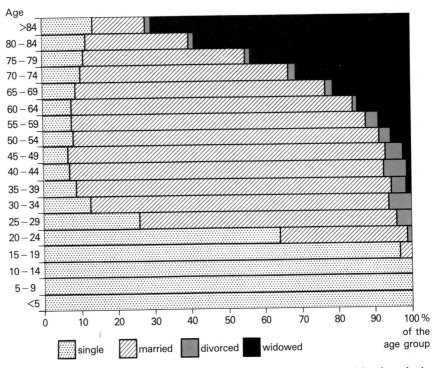

particularly Western and Christian societies, all but a fraction of reproduction is undertaken by persons who are married. However, three points need to be stressed. First, even in those societies which recognise the institution of marriage, an increasing number of people are living together and raising families without getting married. Secondly, there are parts of the world where marriage occurs only when the fertility of a couple has been proven. Thirdly, there are still other areas where marriage *per se* does not exist.

In those societies committed to the institution of marriage, marital status is a significant influence on such demographic aspects as fertility and population growth. As far as fertility is concerned, the critical factor is not the number of fertile women, but rather the number of women of reproductive age who are cohabiting with a man. Marital status is conspicuously age-related. Children and adolescents tend to be single; young adults and adults tend to be married; divorce seems to be greatest amongst those in their 30s (divorce amongst those over 40 appears to be less numerous, largely by

reason of remarriage); and widowhood is concentrated amongst the elderly (Fig. 5.14). Another critical aspect is the age of marriage; this varies not only from country to country, but also from time to time. In England and Wales, the median age at marriage is currently 25 for men and 21 for women; at the beginning of the century, the ages were 27 and 25. In India, the median ages are now 19 and 17; they were virtually the same in 1900. Clearly, the earlier marriage is contracted, the greater is the likelihood that a couple will produce more children; so the general trend towards earlier marriage is likely to boost fertility. The validity of these broad generalisations is reduced, of course, where birth control is rigorously practised.

A general change in the age of marriage, as experienced in Great Britain, is not the only significant recent trend in marital status. Figure 5.15 shows that there has been a marked increase in the incidence of divorce. Here, as in other Protestant countries, its legal procedures have been made easier, and there has been a change of attitude towards it. Even more

Figure 5.15 *Marriage, remarriage and divorce rates in Great Britain (1961–1985)*

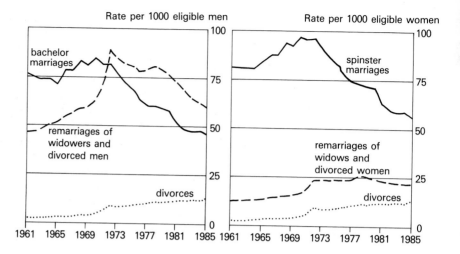

striking has been the decline in 'bachelor' and 'spinster' (i.e. first-time) marriages. This implies that increasing numbers of eligible people are preferring either to live alone or to cohabit as common law husband and wife. Official statistics indicate that the occurrence of widowed people, who are predominantly women, has remained fairly constant in Britain throughout the same period. Of course, their number (as indeed the number of divorced people) is reduced by remarriage, the incidence of which shows a curious divergence as between the sexes (Fig. 5.15).

These changes, particularly in divorce, marriage and cohabitation rates, not only have demographic implications. In Britain, as elsewhere, they have quite profound consequences in rather more practical ways. For example, they affect the demand for housing, both in terms of overall volume and type. The changes experienced in Britain have increased the number of households relative to the size of the population. Since more people are now living on their own (by choice, divorce or bereavement), so more dwelling units are needed. Such people, except possibly single-parent families, do not require spacious family homes; their needs are for compact accommodation. These changes in marital status therefore pose problems to local authorities and their planning departments whose task it is to manage the housing stock as a whole. They also pose a

challenge to private developers who need to judge the market and be disposed to provide the specific types of housing in demand – be it flats, maisonettes or retirement homes (Fig. 5.16).

Family and household size

The next variable is in some ways linked to marital status and it, too, has implications for housing. First, it is necessary to distinguish between *family* and *household*. A household is simply a group of people living together or a single person living alone. A family is a social group based on marriage (or a common law partnership), united by kinship ties and a common culture, and living together as a household. It is common to distinguish further between a *nuclear family*, which comprises a married couple and their children; and an *extended family*. This might comprise several generations of the same nuclear family or people who are related in some way, be it by descent or marriage. Thus, whilst all families are households, not all households involve families. From this it follows that changes in the family can affect the number of households.

In Britain, as in most Western countries, there has been a general decline in the incidence of extended families and an associated rise in the proportion of nuclear families. Increased divorce and the advent of more

Figure 5.16 *Sheltered housing for the elderly*
The silvering of the populations in Stage 4 countries and the breakdown of the extended family in many of them, are creating a particular housing demand. This is for accommodation designed and equipped specifically to meet the needs of the elderly. Amongst the provision being increasingly made, by local authorities, private companies and housing associations, is what is generally referred to as sheltered housing *– wardened accommodation usually involving self-contained units, but with shared use of facilities such as common rooms, gardens and sick bays.*

single-parent families, together with the fact that elderly people are living longer and often alone, have also served to increase the number of households. For example, whilst the total population of Great Britain increased by only 4.5 per cent between 1961 and 1981, the number of households grew by 35 per cent, and the average household size contracted from 3.5 to 2.7 people. Also contributing to this contraction was a reduction in the average number of children per family; it is now less than two.

A household survey undertaken in England and Wales in 1986 showed that, whilst married-couple households accounted for 60 per cent of all households, more than half of those did not contain any dependent children. In many instances, reflecting the persistently low birth rate, the marriage had never or not yet produced children; in other cases either the offspring had left the parental home or they had become financially independent. The numbers of one-person and single-parent households have also shown a marked increase over the last 25 years, and in 1986 they accounted for 25 per cent and 9 per cent respectively of all private households.

These reductions in both family and household size are the outcome of a blend of quite fast-moving social changes. Such changes are to do with shifts in attitudes about children and divorce, as well as changing opinions about family life and life styles generally. Figure 5.17

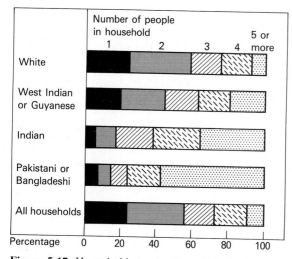

Figure 5.17 *Household size in Great Britain, by ethnic group of head of household (1985)*

might lead us to suspect that these changes might only have affected the White community in Britain. Equally, it may be that their impact on the other ethnic groups has been masked by the fact that such groups were formerly characterised by even larger households (and families). Whatever the case, it is clear that changes such as the increase in the number of households and the reduction of family and household size have important implications, particularly in the context of housing. They alter the overall demand for housing, as well as the amount of space that is required in a dwelling unit.

Socio-economic status

Those changing attitudes and opinions are often closely linked with social class and *socio-economic status*. The latter is determined principally by the type of occupation and the level of income. There is evidence to suggest that differences in socio-economic status are reflected in differences in life styles and values. It is these aspects that can impinge on demographic characteristics, often through the medium of diet and personal health. The last two will certainly have some influence on mortality rates. Unfortunately, vital rates which are

analysed by social class are rarely published. Figure 5.18 gives hints of some differences relating to fertility. In Figure 5.18a, there would appear to be class differences in terms of the interval between marriage and the birth of the first child; it is greatest where the husband is a professional person, and least where he is unskilled. Figure 5.18b indicates that there are class differences as regards family size.

These possible associations between socio-economic status and vital rates assume a geographical significance because of the widespread tendency for social groups to become residentially segregated, in much the same way as ethnic groups (see p. 105). Clearly, where a particular social group becomes concentrated, so too will its associated demographic characteristics – be they relatively high birth rates or relatively low death rates. The type of social segregation commonly encountered in cities of

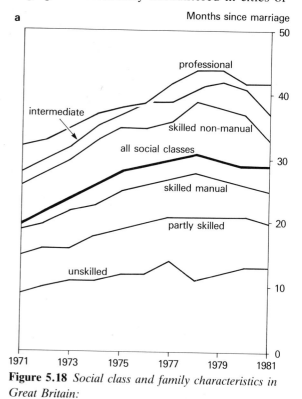

Figure 5.18 *Social class and family characteristics in Great Britain:*

(a) *median interval between marriage and first live-birth, by social class of father*

Figure 5.18

(b) *live-births per family, by social class of father*

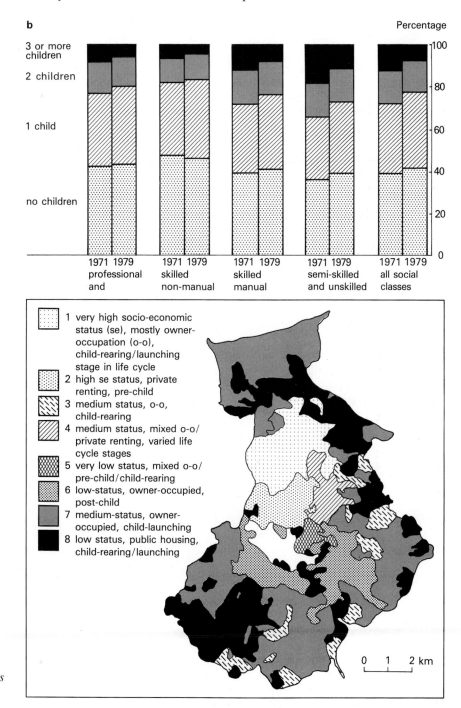

Figure 5.19 *Social areas in Bristol*

the developed world is well demonstrated in Bristol. In addition to socio-economic status, the analysis portrayed in Figure 5.19 takes into account two other closely related variables: stage in the *life cycle*, and dwelling tenure. The former is a significant influence on fertility and mortality rates, and may well help to reinforce the impact of socio-economic factors on those

Figure 5.20 *Social contrasts in the countryside*
*Social polarisation and segregation are as much in evidence in the country as they are in towns and cities. In villages, as here in Hampshire, the social gradients can be quite abrupt, with large detached owner-occupied housing (**a**) juxtaposed with estates of small council housing (**b**). Such segregation can exert a strong local influence on the spatial patterns of demographic variables.*

rates. Dwelling tenure is significant as regards housing conditions, which in turn influence mortality, particularly infant and early childhood rates (see p. 160). Finally, the point needs to be made that social segregation is not confined to towns and cities. The sought-after, upper middle-class 'vodka and volvo' belts of the British countryside may be distinguished from the working-class tracts of tied cottages and council estates (Fig. 5.20). These rural social areas, like their urban counterparts, may also be distinguished in demographic terms.

Place of residence

This distinction between rural and urban areas is also a significant influence on demographic attributes. In the developed world, urban populations are characterised by relatively low birth rates. This is due to the more widespread practice of birth control, and the general perception that children are a drain on financial resources and an impediment therefore to social advancement. Rather different attitudes towards children prevail in traditional rural areas. Proportionately, there tend to be more women in full-time employment in towns and cities, and this also helps to depress the fertility level. Mortality rates are usually higher in urban areas. The greater pace and stress of urban living take their toll; the high population densities encourage the transmission of contagious diseases; there is greater environmental pollution, and the urban environment seems to provoke a higher rate of accidental deaths. Mortality rates would be higher were it not the custom for quite large numbers of urban people to retire to rural areas. Thus the combination of low fertility and high mortality means that the age pyramids of urban populations in the developed world tend to bulge in the middle. This feature is given further emphasis by the fact that it is those in the economically-active age group who constitute the bulk of rural-urban migrants.

The urban populations of the developing world show some of the same demographic characteristics. Mortality rates are relatively high, being raised here rather more by the incidence of poverty and poor housing (Fig. 1.12, p. 23). Rural-urban migration shows the same broad age composition, but the volume is greater. Not unexpectedly, the presence of so many people in the reproductive age-range, together with the general absence of birth control, raise fertility rates to levels far higher than prevail in cities elsewhere. Another point of difference is the virtual absence, as yet, of the urban-rural migration flows and decentralisation increasingly encountered in the larger cities of the developed world.

ASSIGNMENTS

9 Study Figure 5.15.
   a. Discuss the demographic consequences of the trends in marital status shown.
   b. What are the other practical consequences of those trends in marital status?
10 Describe and explain the differences between ethnic groups shown in Figure 5.17.
11 Write an analytical account of the information contained in Figure 5.18.
12 Suggest how and why the following might affect fertility and mortality rates:
   a. socio-economic status
   b. stage in the life cycle
   c. housing tenure.

CONCLUSION

The study of population structure is salutory, if only to remind us of the immense diversity of the human population. But some might argue that a vertical view of population, for that is what it involves, is demography rather than geography. To the geographer, however, the human diversity in population structure is of triple significance. First, the different attributes encompassed by population structure provide various criteria for distinguishing between populations. For example, age structure allows us to distinguish between progressive, regressive, stationary and intermediate populations. Secondly, those same attributes often provide some of the explanation for spatial variations in vital aspects of population. For instance, variations in fertility rates can be related to variations in age structure, sex ratios, marital status, ethnicity and socio-economic status. Finally, population structure is a dynamic phenomenon; it is constantly changing. Many of those changes and their associated trends have spatial consequences. In the contexts of housing and welfare, for example, trends in household and family size, marital status and age structure raise the key questions – what has to be provided and where?

6

The Geography of Hunger and of Plenty

Much of the illustrative material used in the previous chapter related to Great Britain. The picture that emerged was one of a nation undergoing demographic and social change. Particularly apparent was the shrinkage of British society into smaller families and households. It was not, however, revealed that these diminished units are increasingly enjoying more of the consumer goods used to measure the standard of living and quality of life. Table 6.1 shows that, by 1987, more than half of British households possessed one car, a washing machine, a deep freeze, a telephone and central heating; and that more than one in three also had a video recorder and a tumble drier. The overall picture of modern Britain is one of material plenty, perhaps even materialistic self-indulgence. But is that plenty equally enjoyed by all Britons? Do other parts of the world enjoy the same level of material comfort?

POPULATION, RESOURCES AND DEVELOPMENT

Trying to answer those questions requires turning the discussion to the relationship between people, resources and development. It is this which, above all else, conditions our standard of living and our quality of life. By analysing this relationship, we can begin to understand the reasons for the striking contrasts that exist in the world today. Contrast, for example, the desperate plight of the poor in Calcutta and the elegant life-styles of the rich in Dallas; or the starving cultivators of Ethiopia and the surplus-producing farmers of the European Community (EC). These contrasts are part and parcel of the geographies of hunger and plenty. Since spatial differences and the relationship between people and the environment are the focal points of modern geography, here surely is a major issue which cries out for investigation by geographers.

Basic definitions

Before looking at the mechanics of the relationship between population, resources and development, we need to be clear as to the precise meaning of certain terms that will recur in the discussion. The term *resource* tends to be somewhat loosely used. Strictly speaking, we should distinguish between *natural* and *human* resources. The former include any features or items of the physical and biotic environments (such as slopes, minerals, soils, trees) that are used to satisfy a particular human need (such as food, energy, housing). Those things only become resources when they are actually exploited and used; prior to that, they are referred to as *stocks*. Technological progress and economic demand are particularly significant in this conversion of stocks into resources. The stocks of oil and natural gas under the North Sea did not become resources until it became possible to undertake deep-sea drilling from mammoth rigs, and until world prices made it economic to do so. A common distinction is made between *non-renewable* and *renewable* natural resources (Fig. 6.1). The former are finite (such as minerals) and their exploitation leads to exhaustion. The latter are of a flow nature and persist or recur over time (examples are solar energy and rain). Renewable resources may be further subdivided into those that remain largely unaffected by human

Table 6.1 *Household consumer durables in Great Britain (1972–1987)*

	(% of households)								
	1972	1974	1976	1979	1981	1983	1985	1986	1987
Home computer	–	–	–	–	–	–	13	17	18
Video . . .	–	–	–	–	–	18	31	38	46
Deep freeze	–	–	–	40	49	57	66	72	74
Washing machine	66	68	71	74	78	80	81	82	83
Tumble drier	–	–	–	19	23	28	33	36	39
Dishwasher	–	–	–	3	4	5	6	7	8
Telephone	42	50	54	67	75	77	81	83	83
Microwave oven	–	–	–	–	–	–	–	23	30
Central heating	37	43	48	55	59	64	69	71	73
Car/van –	43	44	45	44	44	43	45	44	44
(– more than 1)	9	11	11	13	15	16	17	18	19
(– Total)	52	55	56	57	59	60	62	62	64

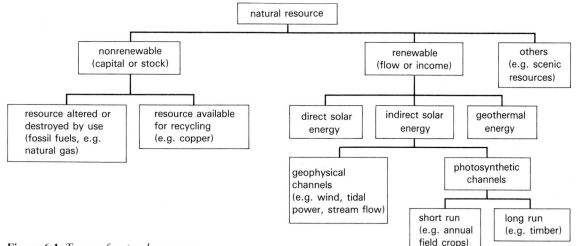

Figure 6.1 *Types of natural resource*

exploitation (wind and tides) and those that are vulnerable to misuse (soils and vegetation). The other major category, *human resources*, relates to certain aspects of people themselves; as, for example, through the provision of labour, their manual skills, their inventive and innovative abilities, or their entrepreneurial talent.

The term *development* refers to the state of a particular society and the processes of change within it. Development is widely regarded as involving progress in four interrelated directions. Two of these are crucial to that conversion of stocks into resources, namely *economic growth* and *technological advancement*. But these are also important to other aspects of change within society, such as urbanisation and industrialisation. The other two dimensions of development are *modernisation*, which is essentially a process of social change (such as changing values, improved social mobility, more efficient social organisation) and *well-being*.

Well-being is a generic term for a group of overlapping concepts, all of which relate broadly to the general condition of a population or society. Amongst these concepts, there is *welfare* which refers to material conditions and embraces such basic needs as food, housing and access to public goods and services (such as education and medical care). *Standard of living* is the degree to which those essentially material wants are satisfied. People may have food and housing, but is that food adequate in dietary terms, and is that housing properly equipped as regards water supply and waste disposal? *Quality of life* is a rather broader concept and takes not only the material side of life into account. It also has a psychological dimension which includes such states of mind as satisfaction, happiness, fulfilment and security. Furthermore, it embraces considerations such as social opportunity, employment and promotion prospects, affluence and leisure. Its assessment is inherently a personal matter, for it really depends on the individual concerned, whereas the assessment of standard of living can be undertaken on a more impersonal and aggregated basis. When measuring standard of living, for example, it is possible to assess with reasonable accuracy the percentage of a given population that has received primary education or that occupies properly-equipped housing.

The distinctions just drawn may appear somewhat slight and clouded. The situation is not helped by the fact the terms are often misused. However, to make matters easier, unless it is absolutely vital to make the specific distinction, the broad umbrella term, wellbeing, will be used thoughout the following discussion. What should also be stressed at the outset is that well-being is widely regarded as one of two important outcomes of the relationship between population, resources and development; the other is environmental use (or abuse). It is these two outcomes, particularly well-being, which provide the themes for the discussion in this chapter and the final chapter.

The concept of optimum population

In analysing the relationship between population, resources and development, it is simplest if we imagine a sort of balance existing between the first two, with the precise nature of that balance strongly conditioned by the state of development (Fig. 6.2). The link

between people and resources is mainly effected through the medium of food supply, the most basic of all human needs. In primitive societies, resource exploitation is largely concerned with bare survival and subsistence. In advanced societies, there are many more options. Resource exploitation might be geared to high levels of food production. Equally, it might involve providing raw materials for manufacturing; in which case the sale of goods, along with the provision of services, will provide the means for purchasing food from elsewhere. Or there might be a mix of these options. In this sense, therefore, development leads to higher levels of resource exploitation which, in turn, raise the *carrying capacity* and therefore the number of people who can be supported. The rise in population, in its turn, becomes a spur to further development, thereby creating a sort of upward spiral. But the spiral does not continue indefinitely; eventually some sort of ceiling is reached.

All this suggests that there always exists a strict equivalence between the number of people in an area and the amount of food that can be raised by whatever means. In reality, of course, there is frequently a mismatch. *Overpopulation* is said to occur when and where the number of people exceeds the supporting capacities of current resource use and the prevailing mode of production. This imbalance most often occurs when population growth races ahead of economic development, as has persisted in China, Indonesia (notably Java), Puerto Rico and many other parts of the world. It can also be caused by exhaustion of nonrenewable resources (as when a coalfield becomes worked out), and by abuse of renewable resources (as when bad farming practices lead to soil erosion), as well as by a decline in the demand for labour. The consequences of overpopulation are painful and are largely reflected in lowered standards of living; the symptoms of this include malnutrition and starvation, increased disease and poverty. Overpopulation can also often be a powerful force motivating migration and civil unrest. Possibly its worst aspect is that its effects are most keenly felt by

Figure 6.2 *A model of some of the relationships between population, resources and development*

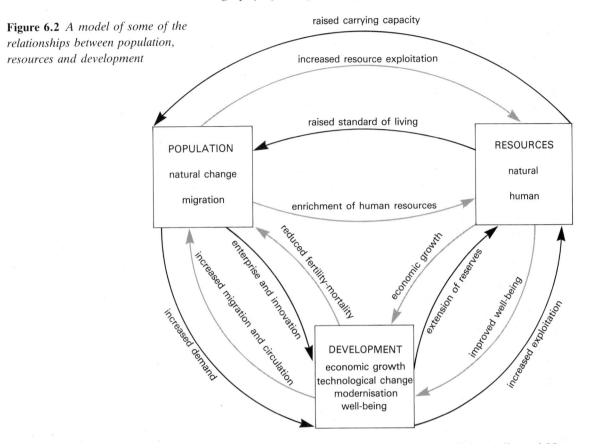

the weakest and poorest members of society. But overpopulation brings environmental as well as human costs. In the desperate bid to raise food supply, there is the irresistible temptation to make short-term gains at the expense of the environment – to overcrop and overgraze and thereby inflict irreparable damage, particularly on soils and vegetation (Figs. 3.15, p. 69 and 7.4, p. 166). Finally, it needs to be pointed out that overpopulation is not necessarily equated with population density. High-density regions, such as the South east of England and the Tokaido corridor of Japan, are no more overpopulated than low-density regions, such as the Andes and the Gobi Desert (Fig. 6.3).

Much less common in the world today is *underpopulation*. This exists where resources and development could support a larger population without any lowering of living standards, or where a population is too small to develop its resources effectively. The former situation probably occurs in parts of Australia and New Zealand where extensive agriculture is capable of supporting quite high living standards. Areas of rural depopulation in Western Europe would also fall into this category. Examples of the latter situation are harder to come by. It is likely to occur where low technical levels prevail (as among pastoral nomads in semi-arid regions); or in pioneer or frontier areas which are being settled for the first time (as in the remoter parts of Siberia and Australia). The consequences of underpopulation, such as they are, can scarcely be regarded as costs in the same way as the consequences of overpopulation.

Between the two extremes of overpopulation and underpopulation, there possibly exists a condition which writers refer to as *optimum population*. This might be simply defined as that size of population which, for a given area, allows the maximum utilisation of resources and achieves the greatest output per capita and

Figure 6.3 *Extremes of population density*
*In Hong Kong (**a**), mean population density exceeds 5250 per km², but can this country be said to be any more overpopulated than the Andean region of Bolivia (**b**), where population density is less than 5 persons per km²? The acid test of overpopulation is whether or not resource development is capable of sustaining an acceptable general standard of living.*

the highest standards of living. It is a critical point on the population growth curve, a narrow divide between underpopulation and over-population (Fig. 6.4a). Clearly, that point will depend on a range of factors, such as the size of the area, the resource base, available tech-nology, the state of economic development and social organisation. Equally, the optimum

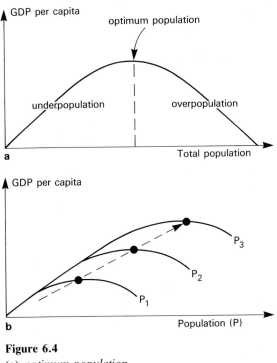

GDP per capita

optimum population

underpopulation   overpopulation

Total population

a

GDP per capita

P_3

P_2

P_1

Population (P)

b

Figure 6.4

(a) *optimum population*

(b) *the effect of improvements in technology on optimum population*

production. Implicit in the model is the idea that adjustments to levels of fertility and mortality will be made before growth reaches the point at which population numbers can no longer be sustained. Adjustments are likely to be made as soon as people become aware that their circumstances are beginning to deteriorate. In other words, that awareness comes, and adjustments are made at point A on the x axis, some time after the community has passed

population will vary over time, particularly with economic growth and technological progress. Figure 6.3b illustrates the double impact of improvements in technology. Of the three curves, P_3 involves the highest level of technology. The optimum population associated with that curve is not only larger than that of the other two curves, it also involves the highest level of GDP per capita (i.e. the highest standard of living). Whether the actual size of an optimum population can ever be accurately identified is very much open to question, but presumably the ideal of achieving an optimum population is something to which governments in all parts of the world aspire.

Wrigley (1967) has produced a model of the relationship between the attainment of optimum population and changes in the levels of fertility and mortality. In its simplest form, the model relates to a pre-industrial society and assumes that material culture is static. In short, it is not possible to secure a steady increase in food

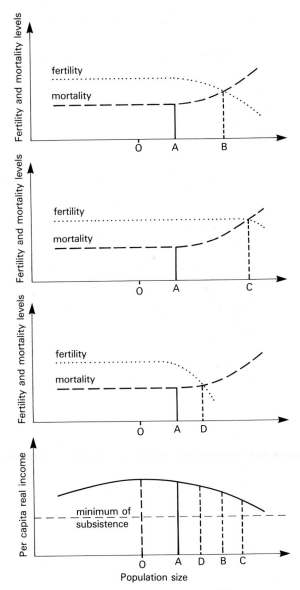

Figure 6.5 *Wrigley's demographic model*

0, the point of optimum population (Fig. 6.5). Clearly, what is critical here is the time it takes to achieve a *stationary population* after point A. The top three graphs in Figure 6.5 show three different demographic situations; the points B, C and D mark respectively the achievement of a stationary population. In the bottom graph, these points are plotted on a standard of living curve. All three occur at different times after A and even longer after 0. What becomes evident is that the achievement is quickest in the case of D (the third graph). It may be reasoned that this form of demographic response, involving a sharp fall in fertility after the point of adjustment (A), is the fastest in attaining a stationary population; this population will, therefore, enjoy the highest standard of living. In short, a stable population is reached before the standard of living curve, shown by the bottom graph, has plunged too far towards the minimum subsistence level that marks the beginning of overpopulation.

ASSIGNMENTS

1 Add to Figure 6.2 by thinking of more links between population, resources and development.
2 Exemplify the effects of overcropping and overgrazing on the environment.
3 Explore what you think might be the consequences of underpopulation.
4 Suggest what measures, other than GDP per capita, might be used to assess the optimum population of an area.
5 Identify the differences between the three demographic situations shown in Figure 6.5.

CHANGING VIEWS ON POPULATION AND FOOD SUPPLY

Many examples may be quoted in support of the idea that the relationship between population, resources and development is conducted mainly through the medium of food supply. The massive emigration of people from Ireland prompted by the great famines of the nineteenth century (Table 4.6, p. 91), or the many thousands who have died of starvation in the Sahel region of Africa during the last two decades are only two cases in point. They and many other instances suggest that there might exist a sort of food supply ceiling, which presumably occurs some time after the point of optimum population. In line with what Wrigley has suggested, the idea might be advanced that, in any given area, population will continue to grow until such time as the number of people reaches that ceiling or *carrying capacity*. Once that ceiling is reached, population growth should level off (Fig. 6.6a). If left to the forces of nature, that elimination of further growth would be caused by starvation and raised mortality. On the other hand, it might be hastened by human intervention in the form of a voluntary reduction of fertility or a mass outward migration. Equally, a stationary population might also be achieved by a combination of all three ways.

The Malthusian view

It was the Reverend Thomas Malthus who, in 1798, first put forward this idea of a ceiling to population growth. He was writing at the time when Britain was beginning to make the demographic transition and experiencing the associated rise in the rate of population growth. He based his theory of population growth on two principles. First, that, in the absence of any checks, human population has the potential to grow at a geometric rate. In other words, population numbers can double every 25 years, so that over a series of 25-year intervals, those numbers will progress 1, 2, 4, 8, 16, 64 and so on. Secondly, that even in the most favourable circumstances, agricultural production can at best be expected to increase only at an arithmetic rate. This means that over the same series of 25-year intervals, the rise in food production may progress 1, 2, 3, 4, 5, 6 and so on. Given the nature of these two growth rates, population

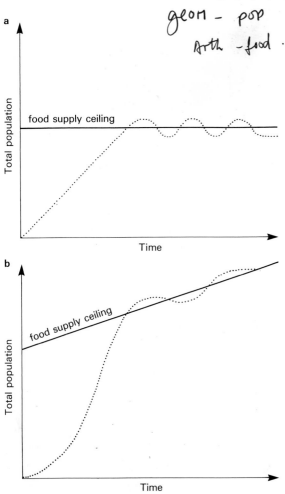

Figure 6.6 *The food supply ceiling:*
(a) *a simple view*
(b) *the Malthus view*

ceiling to be inclined, rising with time, as in Figure 6.6b.

'I think I may fairly make two postulata. First, That food is necessary to the existence of man. Secondly, That the passion between the sexes is necessary and will remain nearly in its present state.'

'Assuming then my postulata as granted, I say, that the power of population is indefinitely greater than the power in the earth to produce subsistence for man. Population, when unchecked, increases in a geometrical ratio. Subsistence increases only in an arithmetic ratio. A slight acquaintance with numbers will shew the immensity of the first power in comparison with the second.'

Quotations from the writings of Thomas Malthus

Malthus suggested that the mechanisms, by which population growth would be curbed as it approached the ceiling, were broadly of two types – *preventive* and *positive checks* (Fig. 6.7a). His main preventive check was what he tastefully called 'moral restraint' as reflected in the decision taken by men to cease 'pursuing the dictate of nature in an early attachment to one woman.' In practice, this meant either celibacy or a delay in the timing of marriage. Provided there was no increase in the number of illegitimate births resulting from the latter, both would reduce the fertility rate. Malthus noted that as food became more scarce and more expensive, this too would tend to delay the timing of marriage. Positive checks to population growth included those things that would raise the level of mortality, such as famine, a lowered resistance to disease caused by poverty and malnutrition, war and even infanticide. The effect of the operation of these checks would be to create oscillations in population growth around the long-term arithmetical increase in food supply (Fig. 6.6b).

growth may be expected progressively to outstrip any increase in food supply. In addition, it is necessary to remember that the rule of *diminishing returns* applies. This states that in any production system, there comes a point in the expansion of the system where output begins to fall relative to rising levels of input. In the present context, this means that any country or region may be regarded as having a finite food-producing potential and this, in its turn, acts as a ceiling to population growth. But the ceiling that Malthus envisaged was not as that shown in Figure 6.6a; assuming an arithmetic rate for the rise in food production, he envisaged the

In some respects, the validity of Malthus's theory has since been reduced by events which were quite unforeseen at the time he was writing. Noteworthy here were the great strides made by the Agricultural Revolution which

Figure 6.7 *Population growth and food supply:*
(a) *the Malthus view*
(b) *Boserup's view*

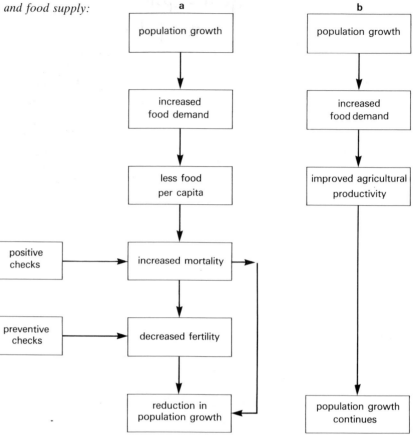

resulted in considerably increased agricultural production. At the same time, the manufacturing base that emerged as a result of the Industrial Revolution provided the means for purchasing food from overseas. This broke the bond between population and domestic food production which was central to Malthus's case. Also, developments in transport allowed food to be gathered from further and further abroad.

There were several demographic developments which Malthus did not anticipate. Improvements in transport also greatly increased the mobility of people and therefore the significance of migration as a mechanism for balancing population and food supply. It might be argued that the huge waves of migration from Europe to the New World during the nineteenth century were illustrative of this mechanism in operation (Fig. 4.15, p. 90). Also unforeseen were the widespread adoption of

birth control and the decline in fertility that seem to be related more to changing social attitudes than to the direct control of food shortages. It is interesting to note that Malthus was strongly opposed to birth control within marriage and never suggested that married people should restrict the number of their children. Finally, and partly for the two reasons just given, his claim (based on the case of the USA) that unchecked population growth is geometrical, was not to be borne out, at least, that is, during the nineteenth century. Ironically, though, the late-twentieth century has yielded increasing instances of national populations doubling within 25 years; examples include Colombia, Iraq, Kenya, Kuwait, Libya and Venezuela. In these cases, it is relevant to ask what has been the impact of growth at a geometric rate on the general well-being of their populations? Broadly speaking, well-being has

Figure 6.8 *Symbols of oil-based affluence, Abu Dhabi*
Widespread ownership of expensive cars and large bank deposits are two indicators of the prosperity now enjoyed by people in the modern oil-producing states. Since the Oil Crisis of 1973, oil has become a powerful currency in the global economic system. Whilst high oil prices have undoubtedly accelerated development and progress in most OPEC countries and enabled the support of larger populations, they have also acted to the detriment of those other developing countries having no such resources and which rely heavily on imports of oil.

been maintained, if not improved, in those countries possessing other resources (notably oil, as in all but one of the above-mentioned countries); such resources have, in effect, been traded on the world's markets for additional food (Fig. 6.8). By contrast, where domestic agriculture has had to carry the burden of feeding the extra mouths, as in Kenya for example, there is no such evidence of improved well-being.

Views since Malthus

Interest in the relationship between population growth and food supply has been re-awakened in the last 25 years or so, probably by the acceleration in the rate of global population growth. We might just examine two different views which have been expressed; those of Boserup (1965) and the Club of Rome (1972). At the outset, it should be stressed that Boserup fails to face up to the fact that food production cannot be increased for ever; the Club of Rome is more realistic and explores a greater range of inter-relationships than just people and food.

Ester Boserup, a Danish economist, has put forward a view that is diametrically opposed to that of Malthus. The essence of her case, based mainly on observations made of Third World countries, is contained in the age-old saying that 'necessity is the mother of invention' and in her own quotation that 'agricultural developments are caused by population trends, rather than the other way round.' In other words, she argued that population growth in many pre-industrial countries, rather than being restrained by food supply, has in fact served as a stimulus to the improvement of agricultural production (Fig. 6.6b, p. 139). She pointed out that as population has increased during the twentieth century, so there has been a shift towards more intensive forms of cropping in many parts of Africa, Asia and Latin America. The point is also made that a similar sequence of events was experienced in Europe at a much earlier date. So a sort of negative feedback loop is envisaged (Fig. 6.9). If food per capita decreases to a value below that desired by the population, there will be a tendency to increase agricultural capital (investment in farm production), so that future food production and food per capita can increase. In many respects, then, this is a much more optimistic view of the relationship between population growth and food supply. Indeed, it may be over-optimistic to the extent that it becomes unrealistic, for it ducks the key issue of whether or not there comes a time when food supply can be increased no further. If the time does come, then what will happen?

In contrast, the Club of Rome (see p. 164) has directly addressed that issue. In a report on growth in the world system, published in 1972 under the title of *The Limits to Growth* (D. L. Meadows *et al*), the members of the Club clearly demonstrated that population growth cannot continue indefinitely. In their so called *world*

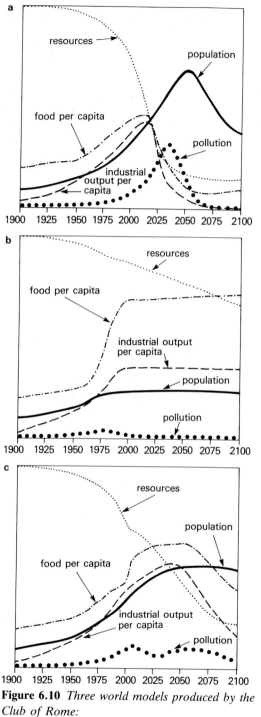

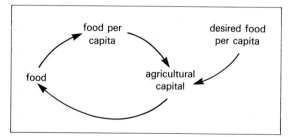

Figure 6.9 *The negative feedback loop associated with food supply*

Figure 6.10 *Three world models produced by the Club of Rome:*
(a) *standard run*
(b) *stabilised*
(c) *stabilising policies introduced in the year 2000*

model standard run, they demonstrated that if the trends shown between 1900 and 1970 (in variables such as population growth, resource depletion, industrialisation and food production) were projected to the end of the twenty-first century, the limits to population growth on this planet would be reached well before that time (Fig. 6.10a). The Club of Rome saw the only hope for the future of the human race to lie in the introduction of growth-regulating policies. These policies would involve regulating population so that births did not exceed the replacement rate, holding the resource depletion rate at its pre-1970 level, doing much more by way of resource recycling, and switching capital investment away from industry into agriculture and services. Had those policies been implemented in 1975, the outcomes would have been as shown by Figure 6.10b. Figure 6.10c shows the future scenario if the introduction of these stabilising policies is delayed until the year 2000. In the face of continuing exponential population growth, attainment of the desired state of demographic, ecological and economic stability becomes increasingly difficult. As of 1990, the prospects do indeed seem gloomy, given the fast approach of the turn of the century and the few signs of intervention so far made to bring about stabilisation.

ASSIGNMENTS

---

6 Justify the claim that the Boserup view of population and food supply is more optimistic than that of Malthus.
7 Critically examine the validity of the assumptions made in drawing up model (a) in Figure 6.10.
8 With reference to Figure 6.10, identify and explain the differences between models (b) and (c).

LEVEL OF LIVING AND STATE OF WELL-BEING

The two geographies referred to in the title of this chapter should not be taken too literally. The terms *hunger* and *plenty* are used in a much broader sense than just food supply. They are intended to convey the basic idea that spatial contrasts exist in the world between areas of shortage and deprivation and areas of surplus and wealth. Admittedly, food supply (its adequacy or otherwise) is a vital aspect of those geographies, but there are many other strands which collectively interact to produce what is generally referred to as well-being. These strands need to be identified, and ideally measured, before we proceed to an investigation of the two geographies.

---

1 *Somatic status* (physical development)
  a Nutritional status
  b Health status
  c Life expectancy
  d Physical fitness

2 *Educational status* (mental development)
  a Literacy
  b Educational attainment
  c Congruence of education with manpower needs
  d Employment

3 *Social status*
  a Integration
  b Participation

Table 6.2 *Composition of Drewnowski' state of well-being index*

Drewnowski (1974) has suggested that well-being is essentially the state or condition that is derived by a population from the consumption of those goods and services provided to satisfy basic human needs, such as food, shelter, medical care and education. Thus the *state of well-being* might be seen as the *output* derived from that consumption of goods and services. He proposed that this state can be measured by an index, the derivation of which is shown in Table 6.2. Basically, three main components are recognised, each being seen as a major facet of human life; these are the physical, mental and social status of people. Of these, clearly the first is the most demographic and relates closest to what has been discussed earlier in this book. The other two, whilst less closely related to our discussion, are clearly important aspects of the quality of life. Drewnowski also defined what he called the *level of living*, measured by a *level-of-living index*. It involves no less than 27 separate measures, relating to such things as nutrition, clothing, housing, health, education, leisure, security, as well as to the social and physical environments. The index is compounded from those goods, services and amenities which exist or are utilised to satisfy human needs and which, when consumed, produce the state of well-being. They might best be seen, therefore, as the *inputs* of well-being.

These two concepts of state of well-being and level of living are brought together in Figure 6.11, where they provide the axes for plotting what Smith (1977) has called a *need satisfaction curve*. Along the y axis, four different states of well-being are defined. The curve shows the inputs or level of living required to sustain a given output or state of well-being. The form of the curve, as drawn, indicates that, as the level of living increases, the impact on the state of well-being is less than proportional. The equal space between A and B and B and C along the y axis is not repeated along the x axis. In short, inputs do not have a directly proportional impact on the output. This may be

illustrated by the fact that once hunger is satisfied, further increases in food supply are unlikely to do much to improve physical status; indeed, there probably comes a point when excessive feeding has a deleterious effect on well-being; hence the eventual downward turn of the curve. In Figure 6.11, the state of affluence is shown as lying above the need satisfaction curve, thereby implying that rising levels of affluence involve increasing degrees of superfluity and excess.

Of the two indices, the state of well-being index would seem to be of more immediate concern to our discussion. After all, it is the outcome (the actual state of well-being) rather than the level of input that is more manifest in the two geographies. Table 6.2 indicates the ten separate measures involved in the compilation of this index. It is from this list that we shall select some of our measures for investigating the two geographies. In fact, the selection is partly done for us, in that worldwide data are not available for all ten criteria. Perhaps most unfortunate is the limited availability of hard data relating to social status. This is due, in part, to the rather elusive nature of the concept; most of us sense its existence, but it is difficult to nail down in concrete terms. It is also due to the inherently sensitive nature of the topic, to the extent that governments often prefer not to collect and publish relevant data. However, data are forthcoming for somatic and educational status. In addition, we shall employ one or other of what are probably the two most widely-used indices of well-being: GNP per capita and GDP per capita. Reference to one of these allows us to monitor what is arguably a fourth dimension of well-being (ignored by Drewnowski), namely the material or *economic status* of people in a given country or region. This status, which closely accords with what is generally accepted as being the standard of living, may be assessed by reference to a number of measures relating to employment and housing. In the ensuing discussion, it is vital to remember that all the measures used are aggregate measures. At best, they can only provide a pointer as to the general state of affairs.

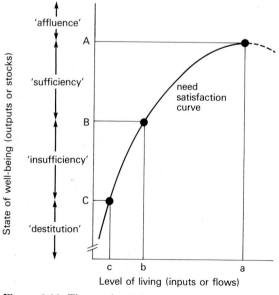

Figure 6.11 *The need satisfaction curve*

ASSIGNMENTS

9 With reference to Table 6.2, discuss what might be meant by 'integration' and 'participation', and suggest how each might be measured.

10 Think of some other examples that illustrate the particular form of the need satisfaction curve shown in Figure 6.11.

INEQUALITIES OF WELL-BEING AT DIFFERENT SPATIAL SCALES

Using criteria relating to the four different aspects or statuses of well-being (somatic, educational, social and economic), this next section will illustrate the existence of inequalities at different spatial scales, ranging from global to local. Those differences in the state of well-being are the *prima facie* evidence for the prevalence in the world today of the two geographies – of hunger and plenty.

Global inequalities

The idea that the world might be broadly divided into two camps, the *haves* and the *have nots*, is nothing new. It is often claimed that these two worlds first became really apparent during the sixteenth, seventeenth and eighteenth centuries as Europeans explored what, for them, were the unknown parts of the world (particularly in the tropics), establishing their colonial empires. The European colonial powers of the time encouraged the development of their overseas territories and what they saw as the improvement in the lot of the native people. They probably believed that they were creating laudable inequalities in well-being, as between their colonies and what they perceived to be the unexplored world beyond. The native people in those colonies no doubt saw the situation in a rather different light. They might have pointed out that highly-developed societies existed long before the Europeans arrived

(the Aztec and Inca civilisations of Central and South America being two such examples) and that previous development in those parts of the world had always been far from uniform. They might also have argued that, because it was essentially exploitative, colonialism amplified rather than reduced the contrasts in well-being between themselves and the colonial powers. A little later, and perhaps less controversially, the Industrial Revolution was to provide a base for the emergence of a two-class global society of a slightly different kind; the industrial and non-industrial worlds. These emerged because the benefits of industrialisation were enjoyed in its temperate cradlelands long before they spread to the tropical world.

It is largely for historical reasons such as these that today we use a whole range of adjectives to describe what might be perceived as a fundamental rift in the world; as between rich and poor areas, as between areas of plenty and of hunger. Many of them have already been used in this book. Terms such as *backward, undeveloped, underdeveloped, least-developed, less-developed* and *developing* have, over the years, been commonly used to distinguish the disadvantaged parts of the world from the other parts, for which one of the adjectives, *advanced, developed* and, in some instances, *overdeveloped*, is normally used. Also entering the vocabulary is the term *Third World*. Whilst this provides a convenient single label for the poor and hungry parts of the globe, the remaining part requires two labels; *First World* and *Second World* are applied respectively to areas of capitalism and socialism. Even more recently, following the Brandt Report of 1980, the terms *North* and *South* have come into common usage in making the distinction between the haves and the have nots.

Although it is widely agreed that today's world may be broadly divided into these two components, there is no universal agreement as to where the dividing line runs exactly. Indeed, attempts to draw a definitive boundary have been very few. One obvious reason lies in the nature of the distinction being made. Whether we base the distinction on *level of development*

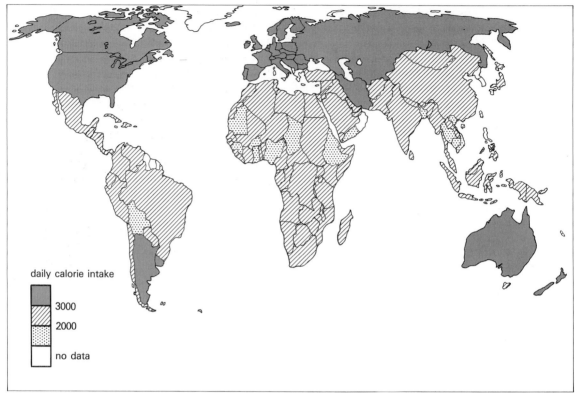

Figure 6.12 *Daily calorie intake, by country (1985)*

or use less economic concepts, such as *well-being* or *human progress*, each is, in its own right, a multi-variate condition. We need to use a range of criteria to measure it properly, and the trouble is that each criterion produces a unique picture. This point is well illustrated if we first compare two maps discussed earlier in this book (Figs. 2.11, p. 43 and 2.12, p. 44) which relate to two possible measures of the physical or somatic aspect of well-being – life expectancy and infant mortality. Whilst the same countries tend to recur in the 'best' and 'worst' categories of both maps, there is clearly a degree of divergence as regards the countries falling in the intermediate categories. If we introduce a new somatic measure relating to nutrition, *daily calorie intake*, it will be seen that a few scattered countries in South America, Africa, the Middle East and South East Asia show values well below the minimum daily requirement of about 2000 calories (Fig. 6.12). At

the other extreme, North America, all of Europe, the USSR, Australasia, together with Argentina and Uruguay in South America, show values well in excess of that threshold. Between these extremes, however, there is much less differentiation than was apparent in Figures 2.11 and 2.12.

Figure 3.14 (p. 68) shows GNP per capita and therefore makes an assessment of the economic status of well-being. Here the eye is certainly drawn to the high values shown by First World countries (unhappily, Second World countries are not always prepared to release their data). Equally, one is impressed by the distinction between most of Africa, South and East Asia on the one hand, with their values below $400, and, on the other hand, Latin America and South East Asia with values often substantially above that level. In short, we are making distinctions here between parts of the world that appeared to be rather

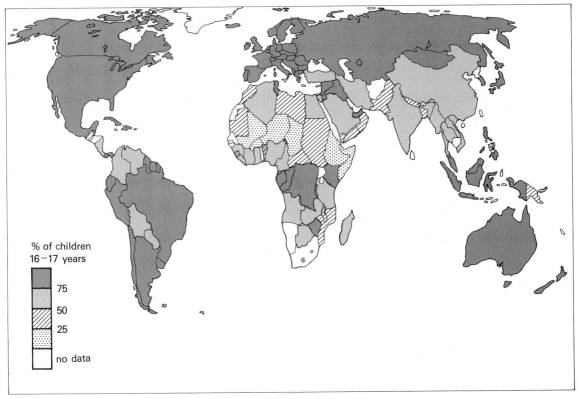

Figure 6.13 *School enrolment ratios, by country (1984)*

similar on the basis of other physical criteria, particularly daily calorie intake.

Moving on to another aspect of well-being, educational status, let us take the *school enrolment ratio*. This refers to the number of children in primary and secondary school, expressed as a percentage of the number of children aged between 6 and 17 years. The picture conveyed by Figure 6.13 is possibly an encouraging one in that quite large areas of the world, which have previously been shown to be in the disadvantaged category, show values greater than 75 per cent. It is only in the northern half of Africa and in scattered parts of the Middle East and South Asia that the ratio falls below 50 per cent.

Figure 6.14 analyses the situation in a rather different way, namely by graphing countries according to four of the measures which we have previously mapped. In each of the scattergraphs, reference is made to two of these measures; in (a) life expectancy is plotted against GNP per capita, whilst in (b), school enrolment is plotted against infant mortality. What is most evident in Figure 6.14(a) is the strong clustering of countries with low GNP per capita and life expectancy values. But the elongation of the cluster clearly indicates the existence of differences even within it. Outside that cluster, there is a wide dispersion of countries along the *y* axis; even so, it might be possible to discern three or four incipient clusters along that axis. Surprisingly, amongst these more affluent countries there are differences of over 10 years in life expectancy.

The pattern shown by Figure 6.14b is even more dispersed. Apart from a clustering tendency amongst those countries combining high school enrolments with low infant mortality, there is a very loose alignment diagonally across the graph. On either side of that line, the eye of faith might find it possible to put tenta-

Figure 6.14

*Scattergraphs showing
the relationship between:*
(a) *life expectancy and
GNP per capita*

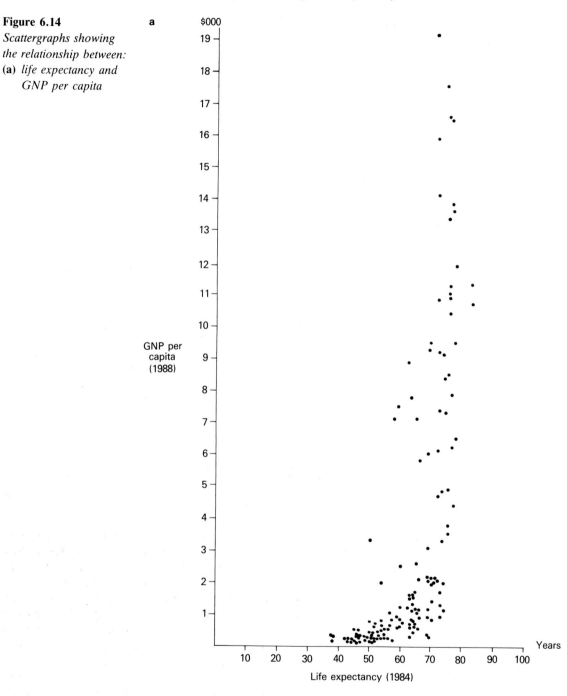

tive lines around some six or seven loose groupings, as for example where infant mortality exceeds 180 per 1000 live-births, or where school enrolments below 45 per cent are combined with an infant mortality rate of less than 120. Certainly, neither scattergraph allows us to identify two distinct clusters, such as would occur if the world were simply to be divided into two clear-cut parts.

Perhaps all this is beginning to become rather

(b) *school enrolment
and infant mortality*

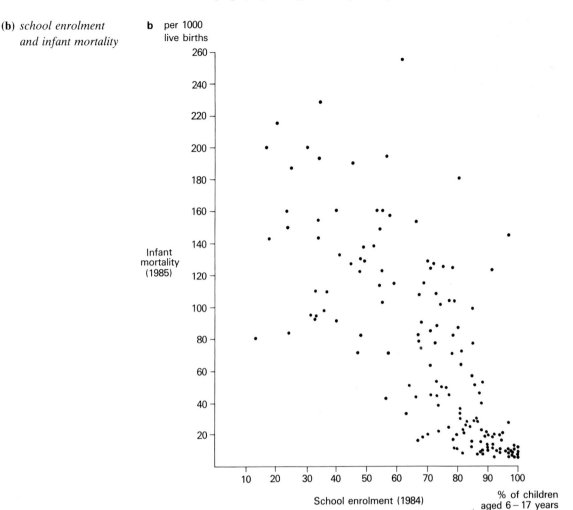

b per 1000
live births

Infant
mortality
(1985)

School enrolment (1984)

% of children
aged 6 – 17 years

confusing, but it should serve to make the following points. First, strong contrasts do exist between different parts of the world when we apply the sorts of criteria employed to assess the state of well-being. Irrefutably, there is inequality at a world scale, and this must be a major concern for society as a whole (see Chapter 7). Secondly, although this contrast between hunger and plenty exists, the world does not break down into two readily identifiable parts. This is partly due to the multivariate nature of well-being, but it is also due to the impact of the processes of development and demographic transition. So we not only have rich and poor countries, but a large number of countries falling into a wide intermediate category; that is, countries which are undergoing economic development and progressing along the demographic transition. These processes mean that the situation is highly dynamic and constantly changing; yesterday's values are unlikely to be the same today. Thus, while it is tempting to use umbrella terms such as *developed world* and *developing world, North* and *South*, we must appreciate that they are dangerous over-simplifications of the real world. And to make distinctions within the developing world, as between *low-income* and *middle-income* economies, or between *least-developed* and *less developed* countries, is only to make a marginal improvement in the accuracy of the generalisations.

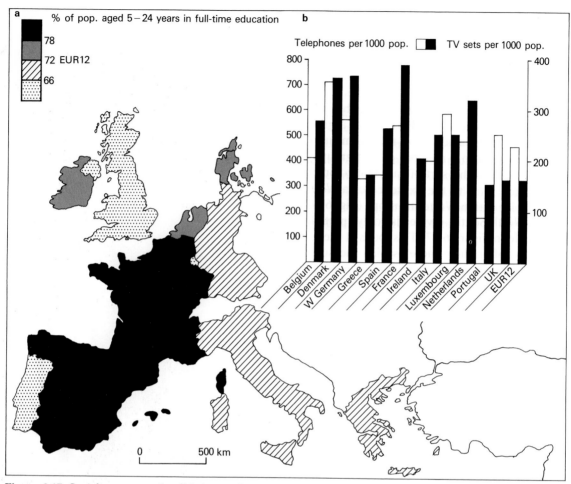

Figure 6.17 *Social measures of well-being in the EC (1986):*
(a) *full-time education*
(b) *incidence of telephones and TV sets*

tion clearly revealed a rift between the Socialist North and the Tory South. Figures 6.18 and 6.19 provide some evidence in support of the basic geographical point that, when the spatial focus is narrowed from the international to the national scale, regional differences in well-being exist in most countries, be they rich or poor. Compared with the global situation, Britain's North-South divide applies the other way round; the division separates an affluent South from the remainder of the country.

In Figure 6.18, the South-east region is shown to have a superior rating in terms of GDP per capita and personal income, as well as in the inverse measure of unemployment. Its prosperity derives from its thriving economy of modern light industry, high-order tertiary services, and quaternary activities. The last two characteristics are illustrated by the relative importance of managerial and professional workers in the south-east's working population. Possibly the maps do not always convey the degree of polarisation that exists in the UK. For example, the rate of unemployment in Ireland is more than twice that in the South-east of England; whilst the GDP per capita and personal income values are at least 50 per cent higher in the South-east. On the

Figure 6.18 *Regional differences in well-being in the UK, using economic measures (1986):*
(a) *GDP per capita*
(b) *total personal income*
(c) *managerial and professional workers*
(d) *unemployment*

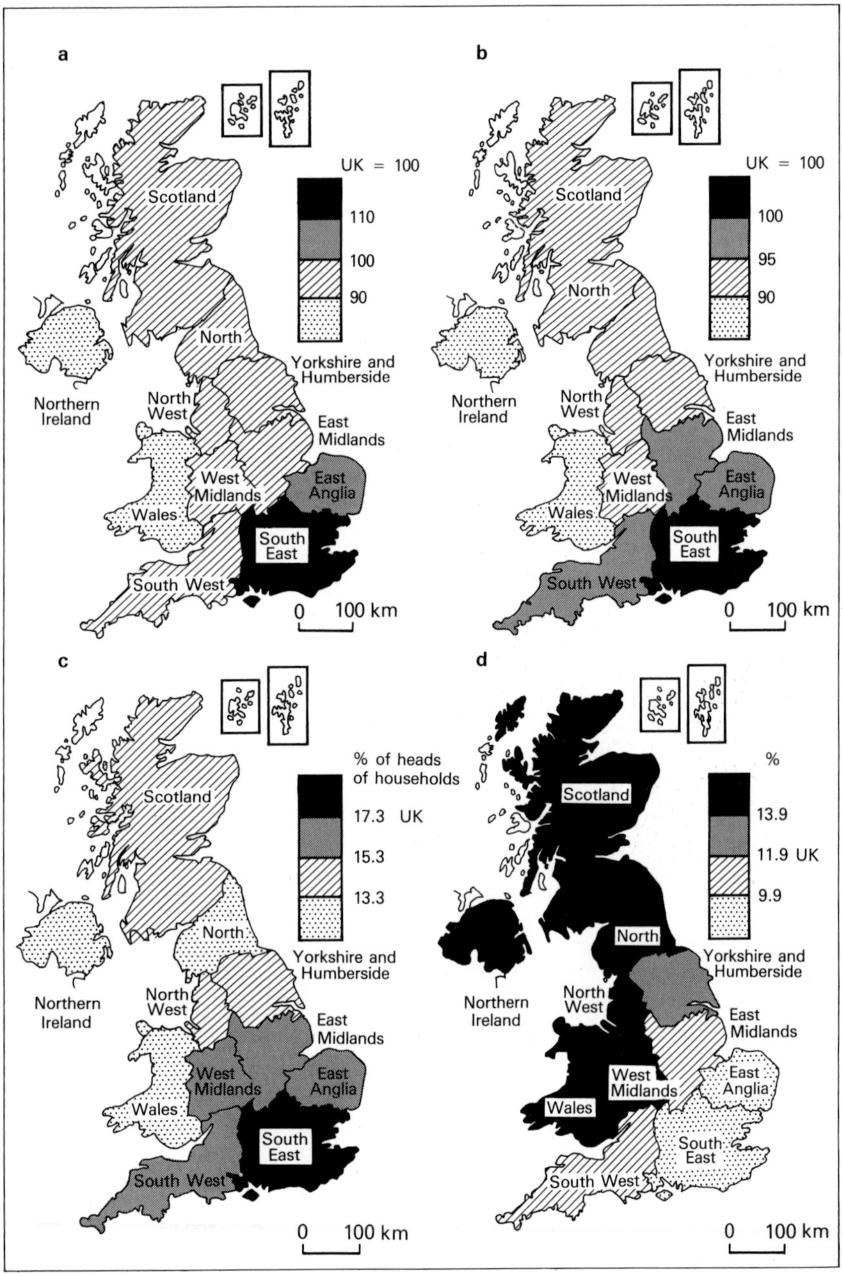

other hand, the maps do convey the impression of a *core* centred on the South-east and reaching out to embrace East Anglia, the South-west and possibly the East Midlands. The remaining regions constitute a *periphery*, within which some variations in well-being are to be detected.

The same general picture is conveyed by the social indices shown in Figure 6.19. These are intended to reflect the four key aspects of health, education, housing and mobility. *Perinatal mortality* refers mainly to miscarriages, enforced abortions and deaths during labour; the map shows a clear distinction between the

153

of the council estates, poverty appears to be rooted in high levels of unemployment, a concentration of single-parent households and an above-average number of sick or disabled persons and elderly people living alone. As for the inner-city areas, poverty is yet another symptom of their *multiple deprivation*. One final illustration of that deprivation and the occurrence of low levels of well-being in a supposedly affluent city is provided by the incidence of *early childhood mortality* (children dying before they reach the age of six). Figure 6.23b portrays data at a sub-ward level and clearly reveals the occurrence of pockets of remarkably high mortality. What emerges is a strong relationship between high rates of childhood mortality and the prevalence of adverse social conditions, such as high unemployment, single-parent families and poor housing.

ASSIGNMENTS

11 Make a detailed comparison of Figures 2.11, 2.12, 3.14, 6.12 and 6.13. Which two maps show patterns which are most alike? Explain why this might be so.

12 Which of the five indicators used in Figures 6.15 and 6.17 do you think provides the best single measure of well-being? Justify your choice.

13 Select one region in the United Kingdom (other than the south-east) and, using data taken from Figures 6.18 and 6.19, analyse its state of well-being relative to the national average.

14 Imagine that you have been asked to investigate the state of well-being in Southampton on a ward-by-ward basis. Explain how you might analyse the data contained in Table 6.3.

15 With reference to Figures 6.16 and 6.24, discuss the factors which give rise to deprived areas within generally prosperous regions and cities.

CONCLUSION

It has not been the purpose of this last section to explain spatial differences in well-being,

rather it has been to demonstrate that inequalities, hunger and plenty, persist at a whole range of spatial scales – from the global to the local. The aim has also been to illustrate that well-being is a multi-faceted condition and that inequalities become manifest in a diversity of forms. These may range from high infant mortality to low school enrolment ratios, from insufficient food to inadequate housing, and from limited personal mobility to poor wages. Also implied in the discussion has been the idea that, in some respects, differences in well-being are relative. Within their respective countries, poor people in Britain are probably no more or less disadvantaged than poor people in Bangladesh. But in absolute terms, the plight of the latter is likely to be considerably worse than that of the former, and no doubt well below what might be defined as the threshold between 'insufficiency' and 'destitution' (Fig. 6.11, p. 144).

As to the causes of inequalities in well-being, these lie rooted in a whole series of spatial inequalities, as for example in the distributions of population, resources, development and opportunity. Other causal factors include differential access to public goods and services, as well as variable balances between people on the one hand and resources, food supply and development on the other. Thus, to a degree, the causes are geographical; but the persistence of these inequalities, no matter at what spatial scale, points rather more to malfunctions within the world's economic, political and social systems. It is these faulty mechanisms that inhibit distribution, access and opportunity. It is these, therefore, that prevent the replacement of the two geographies of hunger and plenty by a single geography of *social justice* and equal well-being.

ASSIGNMENTS

16 Give examples of some of the 'faulty mechanisms' inhibiting a more equal distribution of well-being.

17 Suggest and justify a definition of *social justice*.

7

The Global Outlook

This concluding chapter pursues and broadens the theme of the previous chapter. The discussion looks to the future and in so doing raises a number of issues. These issues are matters of great concern, not just for students of population geography, but for anyone who cares about the world, its people and the future. The issues are immense and complex, but we should not use this as an excuse for ignoring them altogether. The issues are pressing; they have to be faced now and must be continually reviewed in the coming decades. The best we can do here is briefly to itemise the issues, indicating what has been officially written about them, and to encourage you to read further and to contribute to the debate. It is hoped that you will even be persuaded to take action. The last might sound somewhat dramatic, but the issues do require the mobilisation of all thinking people. They relate to such simple questions as; 'What are the prospects for global well-being in the twenty-first century?' 'Is the prognosis one of general improvement?' 'Are there any limits to the possible raising of well-being?' 'Can we expect any reduction of present inequalities, particularly as between developing and developed nations?' As with most questions, answers need to be prefaced by the phrase 'It all depends. . .'. Here, the critical caveat relates to anticipated rates of population growth and projected future levels of population.

POPULATION PROJECTIONS

Some time during the summer of 1987, the global population passed the five billion mark, and this meant that the number of people in the world had doubled since 1950. According to forecasts published by the UNO in 1988, the world population is projected to reach 6.1 billion in the year 2000 and 8.2 billion in 2025 (Table 7.1).

It has been estimated that in 1985 approximately 25 per cent of the world's population lived in the more-developed regions; 35 years previously that figure had been 30 per cent. That implies a significant increase in the proportion of population residing in the less-developed regions (Fig. 7.1). This trend is projected to continue, whilst the rate of population increase in less-developed regions remains at least three times as high as that in the more-developed regions (Fig. 7.2). By the year 2000, 80 per cent of the total population will be resident in parts of the world currently classified as less-developed, and the proportion is expected to increase to 85 per cent by 2025 (Fig.7.1). Clearly, this shift in the overall distribution of population has serious implications in terms of the future prospects for the well-being of the vast majority of the human race.

Table 7.1 and Figure 7.2 show that there has been a slowdown in the rate of world population growth since 1970. This is forecast to continue into the twenty-first century, in both the more- and less-developed regions. By 2025, the global rate is projected to be below 1 per cent. At face value, this reduction would appear to be encouraging. It has to be remembered, however, that whilst growth rates may decline, population numbers continue to grow. Furthermore, the number of extra people in the world each year (which is the product of growth rate and population size) continues to increase. In the period 1950 to 1954, the average annual increment in the world's population was 47

Table 7.1 *World population and mean annual growth rates (1950–2025)*

Year	Population (millions)	Mean annual growth rate over 5 year period (per cent)			
			World	**More-developed regions**	**Less-developed regions**
1950	2516	1950–1954	1.79	1.28	2.04
1955	2751	1955–1959	1.86	1.27	2.13
1960	3019	1960–1964	1.99	1.19	2.34
1965	3335	1965–1969	2.04	0.87	2.53
1970	3693	1970–1974	1.97	0.89	2.39
1975	4076	1975–1979	1.75	0.75	2.11
1980	4450	1980–1984	1.67	0.64	2.01
1985	4837	1985–1989	1.63	0.60	1.94
1990	5246	1990–1994	1.58	0.56	1.88
1995	5678	1995–1999	1.51	0.52	1.78
2000	6122	2000–2004	1.38	0.45	1.62
2005	6559	2005–2009	1.27	0.39	1.48
2010	6989	2010–2014	1.18	0.36	1.37
2015	7414	2015–2019	1.07	0.31	1.24
2020	7822	2020–2024	0.96	0.29	1.10
2025	8206				

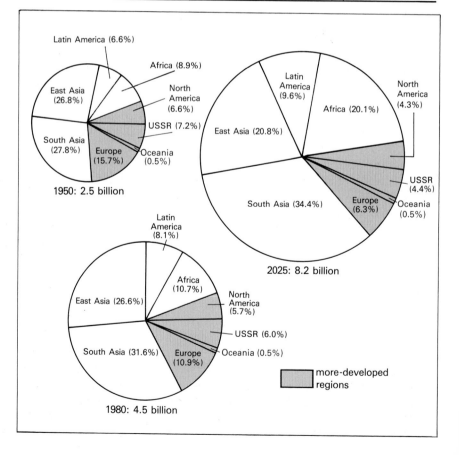

Figure 7.1 *Percentage distribution of world population, by region (1950, 1985 and 2025).*

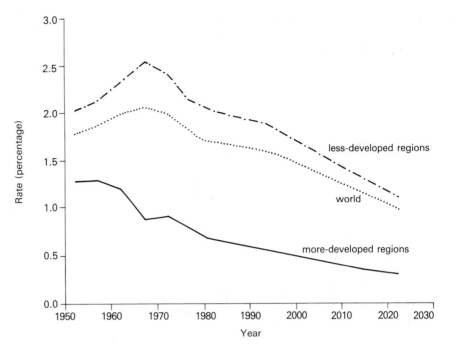

Figure 7.2 *Mean annual rates of population growth for the world, more-developed and less-developed regions (1950–2025)*

million; in the period 1980 to 1984 this had risen to 77 million. The size of the annual increment is expected to reach a peak of 90 million a year near the year 2000, and then fall back to 77 million during the period 2020 to 2024. Again, the point needs to be stressed that the bulk of this population growth will occur in those regions of the world where the current ability to support more people is, to say the least, distinctly limited. In these regions, the prospects of raising the persistently low living standards are indeed bleak.

Given the declining growth rates, the key question is when can we expect the world's population to stabilise? In other words, when will there be zero growth? The short answer is, when fertility rates fall to *replacement level* (slightly over two children per couple). If that critical level were to be reached as early as 2000, the world population would still not become stabilised until 2050, when it would number about eight billion. There will always be this lead time between reaching replacement-level fertility and the attainment of zero growth. However, it now seems more likely that the critical level will not be reached until

2065, and the global population will not become stabilised until 2100. By that time, the world's population will number in the order of 14 billion. These projections clearly indicate the need to take action now. Policies are urgently required to hasten the decline in growth rates and the lowering of fertility levels. Failure to take action today could make a difference of billions to the global population of the next century. But even if effective policies are speedily introduced, and the world population stabilises at a figure of around 10 billion, the vital questions remain. 'Can the world support a population of this size at an acceptable level of well-being? Can this level of well-being be sustained without irreparable damage being inflicted on the global resource base and the environment?'

ASSIGNMENTS

1 Analyse the regional changes in the distribution of the world's population, as shown by Figure 7.1.
2 On the basis of the evidence contained in Figures 3.14 (p. 68) and 7.1, identify the region which you think is likely to experience the most serious

population problems by the year 2025. Discuss the reasons for your choice.

3 Explain why there will always be a time-lag between reaching replacement-level fertility and the attainment of zero growth.

LIMITS TO GROWTH

It was not until the early 1970s that any official concern was expressed about the gathering rates of global population growth (shown in Figure 7.2) and their implications for future well-being. Although some academics had been trying much earlier to awaken political leaders to the potential future problems, it was the Club of Rome (see p. 142) who first captured the attention of some governments. Founded in 1968, the Club of Rome is an informal grouping of experts, drawn from different fields and different countries. Their main purpose was to foster a better undertanding of the varied but interdependent components – natural, economic, social and political – that make up the global system in which we all live. The intention was to bring that new understanding to the attention of policymakers and the public worldwide. By this means, it was hoped to promote policies and actions better able to cope with the problems associated with the current population explosion and its impact on the rest of the global system.

As a result of a meeting of the Club of Rome in 1970, an international investigative team was established under the direction of Professor Dennis Meadows. They were asked to analyse the five basic factors that determine, and therefore ultimately limit, growth on this planet: population, agricultural production, natural resources, industrial production and pollution. Their findings, published in 1972 under the title *The Limits to Growth*, drew three main conclusions. First, as already indicated on p. 143, the report concludes that if present growth trends in world pollution, food production and resource depletion continue unchanged, the limits to population growth on this planet will

be reached some time within the next 100 years. The most probable result of reaching this threshold will be a sudden and uncontrollable decline in industrial capacity and population. The anticipated scenario will not be so different from that forecast by Malthus 200 years ago. Secondly, the conclusion is that it is possible to alter these growth trends and to establish a condition of ecological and economic stability that is sustainable far into the future; that it is possible to achieve a global equilibrium in which the material needs of every person are satisfied (Fig. 6.10, p. 142). Thirdly, the point is made that if people decide to strive for the second rather than the first outcome, the sooner they do so, then the greater will be the chances of success.

It may have been the Club of Rome's report that prompted the United States Government five years later to launch its own study of the probable changes in the world's population, natural resources and environment through to the end of the century. In 1982 its findings were published in a massive three-volume work entitled *The Global 2000 Report to the President*. Its main conclusions were:

'If present trends continue, the world in 2000 will be more crowded, more polluted, less stable ecologically, and more vulnerable to disruption. Despite greater material output, the world's people will be poorer in many ways than they are today. . . . Vigorous, determined new initiatives are needed if worsening poverty and human suffering, environmental degradation, and international tension and conflicts are to be prevented. There are no quick fixes. The only solutions to the problems of population, resources and environment are complex and long-term. . . . If decisions are delayed until the problems become worse, options for effective action will be severely reduced.'

Possibly the most valuable contribution of the *Global Report 2000* is its cataloguing and spelling out of the problems that will ensue if present trends persisted, and if national policies regarding population stabilisation, resource conservation and environmental

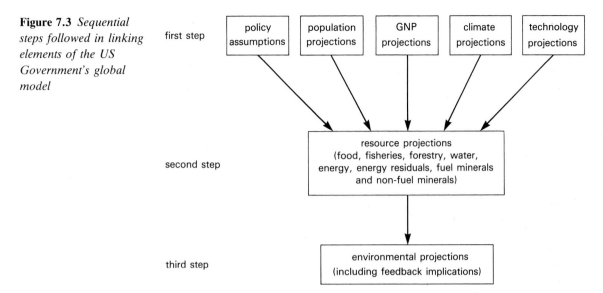

Figure 7.3 *Sequential steps followed in linking elements of the US Government's global model*

first step

| policy assumptions | population projections | GNP projections | climate projections | technology projections |

second step

resource projections
(food, fisheries, forestry, water, energy, energy residuals, fuel minerals and non-fuel minerals)

third step

environmental projections
(including feedback implications)

protection remain essentially unchanged through to the end of the century. The problems identified when following the sequential steps shown in Figure 7.3 include the decline in per capita food consumption in the less-developed countries, serious worldwide deterioration of agricultural soils, climatic change induced by atmospheric concentrations of carbon dioxide and ozone-depleting chemicals, extinction of plant and animal species, and increasing difficulties in meeting energy needs (Fig. 7.4). But above all, the Report, like that produced earlier by the Club of Rome, anticipates that, unless action is taken and changes made, the world's population will, at some time during the twenty-first century, begin to exceed the globe's carrying capacity.

What has been achieved since the publication of these two reports? Apart from the modest slow-down in the rate of world population growth and, in some regions, a growing awareness of the environment and of the finiteness of resources, less has been accomplished than would be needed to achieve a stabilised world population by 2050. Presumably, the first modest achievement will slightly delay reaching the limits to growth, the global carrying capacity. But overall, the steps taken during the 1980s were alarmingly disappointing.

Whilst past 'prophets of doom' have often

been proved over-alarmist, it would seem unwise to rely upon future technology extending those limits and raising that carrying capacity by the same amount as the technological advances of the last 150 years. It is here that one must criticise the *Global Report 2000*. It makes the highly questionable assumption that rapid rates of technological development and adaptation can be sustained well into the future. The grounds for such optimism would seem to be slight. Surely, it is wiser and safer for us to assume that there are finite limits to growth and to act accordingly. To optimistically persist that new technology will bail us out and cope with increasing levels of population is taking a gamble. It is folly to assume that new resources and further reserves can be discovered in harmony with the continuing rise in population numbers.

Similarly, there are grounds for criticising something else implied in both reports, namely that there should be some reduction of the global economic growth rate. At face value, this might appear an attractive and eminently sensible proposal; at least to people in those parts of the world that already enjoy a comfortable standard of living. It has to be said, however, that such a notion is much less appealing to those countries where mass poverty prevails. Here, they would argue that

Figure 7.4 *Gully erosion in Somalia*
In many parts of the Third World so great is the demand for food that primitive farming practices are forced to reap short-term gains without due regard to the longer-term consequences. But by failing to limit livestock numbers and to indulge in arable practices that protect and conserve the soil, irrevocable environmental degradation, such as this large-scale gully erosion, can quickly follow.

increased economic growth is essential if there is to be any real improvement in living conditions and if the vicious circle between poverty and environmental stress is to be broken (see the next section).

These critical observations on future technology and future economic growth serve only to stress that, when it comes to safeguarding the future of the human race, there really is only one option – to curb population numbers.

ASSIGNMENTS

---

4 Explain and illustrate the links shown in Figure 7.3.
5 Examine the likely geographical consequences of the world's population exceeding the global carrying capacity.

SUSTAINABLE DEVELOPMENT AND CONSERVATION

Although there are grounds for criticising some aspects of the *Global Report 2000*, the book did help to sharpen the focus of the global-issues debate. It clearly put the spotlight on projected resource exploitation and on the environmental consequences of that increased exploitation. When this century began, neither people nor technology had the power to radically alter planetary systems. As the end of the twentieth century approaches, not only do vastly increased numbers of people and their activities possess that power, but we are also faced with major unintended changes that are occurring in the atmosphere, in soil, in water, among plants and animals, and in the relationships between them all. These changes taking place in the biosphere are outstripping our present ability to cope with the causes of the problems.

In 1983 the Secretary-General of the UNO asked Norway's Prime Minister, Mrs Brundtland, to put together an independent commission to look further into these particular changes and the issues they raise, and to suggest ways which would allow the world to meet the basic needs of its rapidly-growing population. In particular, this commission was asked to look at the grim and persistent relationship between development and the squandering of resources. Four years later, the group published a report entitled *Our Common Future*, now more commonly referred to as the *Brundtland Report*.

More than the earlier reports so far considered, the *Brundtland Report* established a clear explanatory link between economy and ecology, specifically between Third World poverty and global environmental deterioration. The central message of the Report, as of earlier reports, is the need for fundamental change if anything approaching a tolerable future is to be achieved. There is a call to change international economic systems, change energy technology, change the procedures for managing *global commons* (oceans, Antarctica, outer space), change away from the present world 'arms culture', and (most basic of all) a downward change in the rate of population growth. The Report also stresses the need to change our attitudes towards resources:

'Never before in our history have we had the capacity for change which we now have, and it is a moral obligation for us to use it appropriately. . . . We must collectively stop using up the earth's ecological capital and begin to draw on the interest we can get from sustainable husbandry of its resources. In order to accomplish this transformation, governments need to do two things. First, they need to make the concept of "sustainable development" central to all planning and activities. Secondly, the community of nations needs to evolve a new, more equitable, international economic structure that begins to narrow the gap between developed and developing countries.'

In the remainder of this section, we shall consider the first of these two requirements. *Sustainable development* is defined as development that meets the needs of the present without compromising the ability of future generations to meet their own needs. In other words, it requires a much less extravagant and much more tightly controlled use of non-renewable resources, together with a more efficient management, and greater reliance on, renewable resources. In a nutshell, the essential password must be *conservation*, and environmental and economic considerations need to be closely integrated in all development planning. The costs of failing to do this are already apparent in various forms of environmental degradation. Perhaps most topical are the widening hole in the world's ozone layer, atmospheric pollution, and the clearance of the world's forests which, by a *greenhouse effect*, is raising global temperatures (Fig. 7.5). This, in turn, is encouraging acidification of the environment, increased desertification and glacial melting. The last of these will raise the global sea-level. This might sound a little far-fetched, but at an early stage even a slight sea-level rise threatens to submerge entire island countries such as the Maldives and deltaic countries such as Bangladesh; Venice is vulnerable, as also are parts of the east coast of Britain. Much less publicised as a form of environmental abuse is the squandering of non-renewable resources such as fossil fuels and minerals. In short, the environmental and economic problems generated by recent population growth and development are bad enough, but unless something is done now, those problems are soon going to assume an even greater order of magnitude and seriousness. To say that we are already sitting on a global timebomb is not to over-sensationalise the situation.

Clearly, action is required immediately, but whose responsibility is it to initiate that action? The short answer is the one given in the

Figure 7.5 *Rainforest clearance and the greenhouse effect*
It is currently estimated that nearly 7 million hectares of tropical rainforest are being cleared each year. Not only is the ecological loss immense and irrevocable, but the clearance is a major contributor to the greenhouse effect. Voluntary organisations, like Friends of the Earth, are striving to draw the attention of the world's governments to the causes and consequences of global warming.

THE GREENHOUSE EFFECT

IF YOU THINK A HOTTER PLANET WILL MAKE THE WORLD A COSIER PLACE... THINK AGAIN.

Friends of the Earth

Brundtland Report; it rests primarily with the governments of the world. Alas, to date, few have taken any real initiatives; economic considerations and business corporations still hold sway. Much has been left to one encouraging development, a growing sector of voluntary organisations broadly concerned with conservation. The Royal Society for the Protection of Birds, the Worldwide Fund for Nature (formerly the World Wildlife Fund), the Friends of the Earth, and Greenpeace are examples of such non-government organisations; these through their growing memberships and increasing financial resources, are now bringing pressure to bear on national governments, chiding them to take appropriate action. Thus, in some developed countries (notably Norway, West Germany, and the UK), a 'greening' of politics is gathering momentum, as these key issues of sustainable development and nature conservation assume a higher ranking on the political agenda. Political parties of all shades are beginning to realise that there is a growing tide of public awareness of, and concern about, the environment; when it comes to vote catching, maybe conservation will now begin to count. One might be sceptical about the motives behind this appearance of 'green issues' in the party manifestoes, but if the outcome is a greater degree of environmental protection matched with sensible development, then do we really need to worry too much about the motives?

The timeliness of this advent of 'green' politics has been neatly and graphically summed up in an article in *The Times* (24 January, 1989):

'This new awareness comes not a moment too soon. Each year in tropical countries a desert forms, the size of Holland and Belgium combined; and a forest the size of East Germany disappears, with irrevocable (and immeasurable) loss of plant and animal species. Worldwide, thousands of lakes and rivers are biologically dead, and there is growing toxic contamination of soils and water. In Mexico City, residents have been advised to jog indoors because of the danger of breathing in the air. Almost 40 per cent of India's land area is degraded beyond productive use. In Poland, only 1 per cent of fresh water is safe for drinking. Even in England's green and pleasant land the claims of bottled water and organic farming no longer contend in vain:'

ASSIGNMENTS

6 Suggest possible examples of what you would regard as *sustainable development*.

7 Explain and illustrate what is meant by *conservation*.

8 With reference to Fig. 7.5,
   a. list the reasons for the clearance of rainforests
   b. identify economic activities which might be sustained in such forests.

9 Identify and discuss specific 'green issues' that arise in your local area.

REDUCING GLOBAL INEQUALITIES

The second requisite set down in the *Brundtland Report* identifies the other, and closely related, challenge facing the world as it approaches the twenty-first century. It relates to the point made on p. 161, namely that the pattern of current population growth is essentially an uneven one, and population projections clearly indicate that it will become still more so (Table 7.1, Fig. 7.1). The greatest increase in numbers is, and will continue to be, concentrated in those parts of the world that are already lagging in terms of development and well-being. Further increments of population in those areas would seem to make inevitable a further widening of the so-called *gap* between them and the more-developed parts of the world. Such increments will serve only to proliferate the poverty that already abounds. That poverty is, in a sense, a form of pollution. The needs of daily survival force poor families to think (and live) on a short-term basis. They over-graze grasslands and over-exploit soils in order to maximise immediate yields (Fig. 7.4, p. 166); they cut down dwindling forests for farmland or for fuel (Fig. 3.15, p. 69). What is rational behaviour for the individual becomes collective disaster. The bottom line to all this is that, since poor people in the Third World depend more than others on natural resources for survival, they inevitably become the first victims of environmental decay; poverty and environmental abuse are inextricably linked in a chain of cause and effect. Clearly, it is in these less-developed regions that the limits to growth will first be reached.

But whilst the less-developed regions struggle to maintain even their present relatively low standards of living, the prospects for people in the more-developed regions, by comparison, seem distinctly rosy. The latter regions are not only better equipped to cope with increased numbers, but the projections clearly indicate that, in the event, they will only be required to support relatively small increments of people. This surely is the foremost global inequality – the mismatch between population growth and the ability to support it. This geographical dichotomy inevitably raises two questions. 'Should anything be done to prevent further widening of the development gap, and if so, what?' With respect to the latter question, one might ask whether or not the more-developed countries are under any sort of obligation (moral or otherwise) to help the less-developed. Is there more that the latter might do in order to help themselves?

This whole issue was taken up by the Brandt Commission in 1977. Initially, the Commission was asked by the World Bank to examine the consequences for less-developed countries of changes in the world economy and international relations, particularly as regards food supply, energy, finance and trade. Their first report was published in 1980, entitled *North-South: A Programme for Survival.* It sets out seven priorities, all of which are consistent with the basic idea that the *North* (the advanced, industrial nations of the temperate world) has an obligation to help the *South* (the less-developed countries of the tropical world). These include a massive increase in the transfer of resources from North to South; making large investments in the South's agriculture and in infrastructural developments; improving the conditions of trade and manufacturing for the South; and producing a global energy strategy which reduces the disadvantages of those countries lacking their own oil resources. In the short-term, the North might help the South greatly by wiping out the immense debts that the latter has accrued as a result of borrowing, at high rates of interest, from the North. The seriousness of the debt problem is illustrated by the estimate made in 1980 that of the $845 billion borrowed by countries in the South, a staggering $837 billion was paid back immediately in the form of interest on existing loans. This left only $8 billion to finance the developments necessary to raise the level of well-being in those countries.

The strategy suggested by the Brandt Commission is therefore one of economic aid to be extended by the North to the South. Certainly, there are grounds for asking whether or not the world's richest nations have been, and are, doing enough in this way. For example, the world's three richest countries (the USA, Japan and West Germany) give development assistance to the Third World valued at less than 0.5

per cent of their GNP. Such a small figure suggests that there is considerable scope for the most affluent countries of the North to do more for the poorest nations. In addition, the point might be made that the targetting of development assistance seems to be influenced by political and economic expediency, rather than absolute need. The USA may be seen as directing its aid rather more towards those developing countries which have a strategic location in terms of defence and global security (such as the Philippines and El Salvador). Analysis of Japanese overseas development assistance, on the other hand, indicates that aid is most forthcoming for those countries (such as Indonesia and China) which are able to offer energy supplies, raw materials, cheap labour or a ready market for Japanese manufactures.

But the question is not simply whether the more-developed countries should do more. There is also the question of what constitutes the most appropriate form of aid. It is critical that the right kind is given. For example, giving aid in the form of food is no real answer to the food shortages and malnutrition that prevail in the South. It is tempting to think of this as a neat solution, given that the North produces massive food surpluses – it has its butter, meat and grain 'mountains', milk and wine 'lakes' (Fig. 7.6). To give or sell this surplus food to the South would, at best, only serve as a short-term stop-gap. In the long-term, it would merely increase the South's dependence on the North and act as a poor substitute for what is really required, namely raised and more reliable domestic food production. To this end, the immediate need is for technical assistance which exploits available (rather than imported) technology; and for systems of food production which can be sustained without inflicting irreparable damage on the environment. In support of this, investment in developing countries should be less in manufacturing and more in the agricultural sector. But that investment should heed the lessons of the so-called *Green Revolution*. In too many developing countries, this has transformed low-energy, self-provisioning, labour-intensive agriculture into

a

b

Figure 7.6 *Food surplus and food shortage – an immoral spatial inequality*
A Breton warehouse full of sacks of dried milk **(a)** *illustrates just one of a range of agricultural surpluses produced in the European Community. In stark contrast, the distribution of the contents of one of those sacks in Central Africa, as part of famine relief* **(b)***, epitomises the shortage of food that prevails in many developing countries. But, even if it could be arranged, would the transfer of First World food surpluses necessarily provide a lasting solution to the plight of starving people in the Third World?*

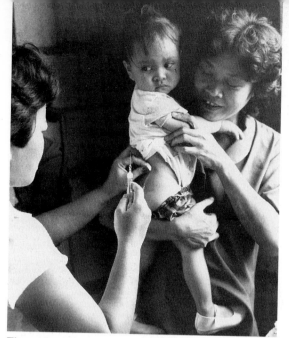

Figure 7.7 *Child immunisation in the Philippines
Immunisation and innoculation programmes in all
parts of the world have done much to reduce infant
mortality. However, the trouble is that higher rates
of survival among young children all too often lead
to higher rates of population growth. Clearly, such
programmes need to be conducted alongside other
programmes which preach the critical message that
greater survival carries with it an obligation to
produce fewer children.*

high-energy, capital-intensive farming which is
dependent upon a wide range of industrial
inputs.

Medical aid is also questionable, since it is
basically concerned with the reduction of
mortality, and thereby exacerbates population
growth. It is worrying that the *Brundtland
Report* attaches so much importance to the
establishment of primary health clinics, as well
as to increasing preventive medicine, improving
water supply, sanitation, etc. (Fig. 7.7).
Medical aid of this type, if it is to be extended,
must be coupled with programmes aimed at
implementing birth control; for reducing
mortality merely lowers still further the level of
fertility required before population growth
reaches its replacement level. This may seem
a rather heartless line of reasoning, but its truth
cannot be ignored.

Thus we might suggest that the aid extended
to developing countries needs to be geared to
three objectives; improving the means of self-
support, particularly in the context of food
supply; educating people in the need to achieve
a sustainable utilisation rather than an over-
exploitation of resources; implementing effective population control.

As regards population control, one might ask
whether the Chinese solution of the one-child
family is too draconian and unpalatable for
others to follow? Can the less-developed countries afford to rely simply on education and
voluntary birth control? Such courses of action
take time to become effective, and basically the
time-scale of the problem is too short. It might
be argued that the *Brundtland Report* is too
soft when it suggests that only some countries
(i.e. those at Stage 2 in the demographic transition) need to limit population growth. Surely,
all countries need to do this in order to reduce
the overall pressure on resources. Also
worrying is the point made in the report that
'an additional person in an industrialised
country . . . places far greater pressure on
natural resources than an additional person in
the Third World.' Whilst that is irrefutable,
such a statement might be easily interpreted as
condoning population growth in the Third
World and condemning it elsewhere. It also
deflects from the basic truth that the global
population problem at the end of the twentieth
century is substantially, but not exclusively,
focused on the developing world.

ASSIGNMENTS

10 Examine the arguments for and against giving
aid in the form of medical services and equip-
ment.

11 With reference to one developing country, examine the achievements and drawbacks of the
Green Revolution.

12 Which of the three aid objectives outlined above
do you think will be the most difficult to achieve?
Justify your choice.

13 What is the reasoning behind the claim made in
the Brundtland Report that 'an additional person
in an industrialised country . . . places far

Figure 7.8 *A new village water supply, Kampuchea*
There can be no doubt that these childern have witnessed a modest but basic improvement in their
well-being. The new well and pump, by providing a more reliable and purer water supply, hold out the
promise to these youngsters of a healthier and a longer future.

greater pressure on natural resources than an additional person in the Third World'?

14 Discuss the issue raised in the caption to Fig. 7.6.

THE CHALLENGE

It is that last point which has possibly given rise to the misconception, held by too many people in the more advanced countries, that the global problem is someone else's worry; that it is something which the developing countries, with their fast-growing populations, limited capital, low technology and pressured resources, have to sort out for themselves. It needs to be stressed, however, that the North, too, has its challenges which are no less urgent. These include: restraining the flagrant misappropriation of scarce resources for non-essential purposes; removing the nonsense of subsidising farmers to produce food that is surplus to requirement; reducing the excessive consumption of fossil fuels; restraining the greater use of nuclear power, and remedying the present abuse of much of our environment. The North also has its spatial inequalities of well-being.

But the root problem that menaces the world today, excessive population growth combined with unsustainable development, is already of such a magnitude, and the situation is deteriorating at such a pace, that our very survival is now at stake, no matter where we happen to live on the globe. We should all be concerned, and we should all be willing to take our share of appropriate action. Besides putting its own house in order, the North needs to provide aid of the right kind and quantity to help the South achieve that critical sustainable balance between population and resources. The South needs, above all, to control its population growth. All governments, North and South, need to be party to international conventions which seek to protect the environment and to promote the right sort of development. Today, we are confronted by a situation that threatens not only the human race, but also much of the biosphere. Failure to act today promises a disastrous tomorrow.

173

Selected references

GENERAL

Demko, G. J. et al. (eds.) (1970) *Population Geography: a Reader* (McGraw Hill).
Haggett, P. (1983), *Geography: A Modern Synthesis* (Wiley).
Small, R. J. & Witherick, M. E. (1989), *A Modern Dictionary of Geography* (Arnold).
United Nations, *Demographic Yearbook*.
United Nations, *Statistical Yearbook*.
Woods, R. (1982), *Theoretical Population Geography* (Longman).
Zelinsky, W. et al. (eds.) (1970), *Geography and a Crowding World* (Oxford University Press).

CHAPTER 1
DEFINITION, DATA AND DISTRIBUTION

Beaujeu-Garnier, J. (1978), *Geography of Population* (Longman).
Dickinson, G. C. (1973), *Statistical Mapping and the Presentation of Statistics (Arnold)*.
McGaugh, M. E. (1970), *A Geography of Population and Settlement* (Wm. C. Brown).
Morgan, W. T. W. (1973), *East Africa* (Longman).
Trewartha, G. T. (1969), *A Geography of Population: World Patterns* (Wiley).
Wijkman, A. & Timberlake, L. (1984), *Natural Disasters: Acts of God or Acts of Man?* (Earthscan).

CHAPTER 2
FERTILITY, MORTALITY AND NATURAL CHANGE

Bogue, D. J. (1969), *Principles of Demography* (Wiley).
Clark, C. (1977), *Population Growth and Land Use* (Macmillan).
Pressat, R. (1972), *Statistical Demography* (Methuen).
Woods, R. (1979), *Population Analysis in Geography* (Longman).
World Bank (1987), *The World Bank Atlas, 1987* (World Bank).

CHAPTER 3
THE DEMOGRAPHIC TRANSITION

Bogue. D. J., *op. cit.*
Broek, J. O. M. & Webb, J. W. (1968), *A Georgraphy of Mankind* (McGraw-Hill).
Clarke, J. I. (1979), *Population Geography and the Developing Countries* (Pergamon).
Davis, K. (1963), The theory of change and response in demographic history. *Population Index*, **29**, 345–366.
Notestein, F. W. (1945), Population: the long view. Schultz, T. W. (ed.) *Food for the World* (Chicago University Press).
Thompson, W. S. (1929), Population. *American Journal of Sociology*, **34**, 959–975.
World Bank (1984), *The World Development Report* (Oxford University Press).

CHAPTER 4
POPULATION ON THE MOVE

Lee, E. S. (1970), A theory of migration. Reprinted in Demko, *op. cit.*, 288–297.

Lewis, G. R. (1982), *Human Migration* (Croom Helm).

Ogden, P. (1984), *Migration and Geographical Change* (Cambridge University Press).

Todaro, M. P. (1976), *Internal Migration in Developing Countries* (International Labour Office).

Zelinsky, W. (1970), *A Prologue to Population Geography* (Prentice-Hall).

Zelinsky, W. (1971), The hypothesis of the mobility transition. *Geographical Review*, **61**, 219–249.

CHAPTER 5
POPULATION STRUCTURE
AND ITS CONSEQUENCES

Bogue, D. J., *op. cit.*

Central Statistical Office, *Annual Abstract of Statistics* (HMSO).

Central Statistical Office, *Social Trends* (HMSO).

Herbert, D. T. & Johnston, R. J. (eds.) (1978), *Social Areas in Cities: Processes, Patterns and Problems* (Wiley).

Knox, P. (1982), *Urban Social Geography: An Introduction* (Longman).

Pressat, R., *op. cit.*

Warnes, A. M. (ed.) (1982), *Geographical Perspectives on the Elderly* (Wiley).

CHAPTER 6
THE GEOGRAPHY OF HUNGER
AND OF PLENTY

Boserup, E. (1965), *The Conditions of Agricultural Growth* (Allen & Unwin).

Boserup, E. (1981), *Population and Technology* (Blackwell).

Coates, B. E., Johnston, R. J. & Knox, P. L. (1977), *Geography and Inequality* (Oxford University Press).

Central Statistical Office, *Regional Trends* (HMSO).

Drewnowski, J (1974), *On Measuring and Planning the Quality of Life* (Mouton).

Malthus, T. R. (1966), *First Essay on Population, 1798* (Macmillan)

Meadows, D. L. et al. (1972), *The Limits to Growth* (Pan).

Smith, D. M. (1977), *Human Geography: A Welfare Approach* (Arnold).

Southampton City Council (1986). *Poverty in Southampton* (Southampton City Council).

UNESCO, *Statistical Yearbook*.

World Bank, *World Development Report* (Oxford University Press) (annual publication).

Wrigley, E. A. (1967), Demographic models and geography. Chorley, R. J. & Haggett, P. (eds) *Socio-Economic Models in Geography* (Methuen).

CHAPTER 7
THE GLOBAL OUTLOOK

Barney, G. O. (1982), *The Global 2000 Report to the President* (Penguin).

Hinrichsen, D. (1987), *Our Common Future: a Reader's Guide* (Earthscan).

Independent Commission on International Development Issues, (1980). *North-South: A Programme for Survival* (Pan).

Independent Commission on International Development Issues, (1983). *Common Crisis: Cooperation for World Recovery (Pan)*.

Meadows, D. L. et al., *op. cit.*

Robinson, R. (1981), *Population and Resources* (Macmillan).

United Nations (1988). *World Population Prospects*.

World Commission on Environment and Development (1987), *Our Common Future* (Oxford University Press).

Index